Forgiveness: A Process Not an Act

Dr. Bernard Kent, Jr.

Cover Design: Brittany Janay Jackson

Published by G Publishing, LLC
P.O. Box 24374
Detroit, MI 48224

ISBN 13: 978-0-9814650-1-2
ISBN 10: 0-9814650-1-3

Library of Congress Control Number: 2008920345

Printed in the United States of America

DEDICATION

This book is dedicated to my parents, Reverend Bernard Kent, Sr. and Ludene Kent, who impacted my life with many levels of experiences that affected me in the growth and admonition of the Lord; to my former pastors, Reverend, Doctor Issac Croom Turner, and Reverend, Doctor Dennis Kidd, for their encouragement along with many other members of the Savannah Church of God. To my grand-parents, John Wesley Miller and Mamie Lee Burns Miller, now deceased, for the Christian foundation upon which so many of my family members continue to strive; and to each of my children, Schenterial, Absolon (Al), Sharnda and Berneta.

Special recognition goes to my sister Bettie Cannon for proofreading and encouragement to complete this project. I would also like to thank my daughter Berneta and son Al for their many hours of editing and revisions.

TABLE OF CONTENTS

INTRODUCTION

Christian believers are bound to Jesus through the process of forgiveness. Through forgiveness believers are no longer at odds with Jesus, but become available to learn of His will with growth and development through the Word. With forgiveness from the Master, Christian believers should respond to one another, keenly aware of their status through forgiveness.

There is no person that is eligible to be so bold that he denies the generosity of forgiveness by Jesus. Therefore, no one should be so unforgiving as not to forgive a repentant brother or sister in the faith. All have come short of the glory, yet forgiveness as a gift from God is so worthy that believers should continue the rotation by extending it to others.

To talk of forgiveness and not put it into practice is of no value. It is an opportunity for an imperfect person who receives forgiveness to extend it to another imperfect person, to have and maintain a relationship worthy of the admiration of our Lord. The Christian believers must keep a relationship with fellow Christians to reach the world. As Jesus forgave all who came to Him in faith, all who come to Him in faith believing on the importance of being forgiven must also practice this process.

To forgive is to relieve one of the debts owed and accept the pain of not receiving what is due. On the cross, Jesus issued the plea, "Father forgive them, for they know not what they do." A Christian believer must never forget his relationship with Christ to forgive and to seek to forgive any person that has done wrong to him. In Mark 11:25-26, Jesus reminds the believer, "Whenever you stand praying, forgive, if you have anything against anyone, so that your Father who is in heaven will also forgive you your transgressions."[1] The consequences of not forgiving are stated in verse 26. "But if you do not forgive, neither will your Father who is in heaven forgive your transgressions."[1] Every person needs the forgive-ness that is available through God by personal relationship. Forgiveness is a channel through which vision for maturity is complete with the Holy Spirit.

CHAPTER 1

Forgiveness

Forgiveness is a process built on relationships. It is more than an act. It is the opportunity for building up within rather than tearing down. Forgiveness accepts personal loss and releases the other person from damages. When one does not forgive, the other person has control. When the non-forgiver is holding someone, pressure, resentment, frustration and dis-fellowship build to effectively maintain separation. One cannot opt away from someone who does wrong. There must be effort within oneself to open to the Holy Spirit to recognize that a healing and cleansing must occur as forgiveness takes place.

Too often the process of forgiveness is not between non-believers and believers. Rather it is between believers and believers. One would think that believers would never disassociate themselves from each other. When they do, believers become a speck in the eye of the sinner prohibiting the sinner from seeing Jesus. When a believer has been hurt by another there must be an opportunity to clear up the problem. If resentment and division becomes the issue, then the person who was wrong or feels that wrong was done must begin a process. This process recognizes hurt, pain, frustration, ego and revenge for himself, and the chance to get even. For a moment in the process, the thought of Jesus comes to mind. I wronged Jesus. I did everything insulting to the Holy Spirit, and yet Jesus, through the Holy Spirit, wants a loving relationship. Jesus loves me and proved it with forgiveness. Am I so much that I cannot extend to have a relationship through the process of forgiveness?

Forgiveness is necessary to maintain unity with believers. How can there be unity with Christ when there is disunity between believers? Matthew 18:35 states: "So likewise shall my heavenly Father do also unto you, if ye from your hearts forgive not every one his brother their trespasses."[2] Forgiveness for the believer begins within. Having been forgiven, there is the urgency or it should be to extend forgiveness.

Many broken relationships exist today because of selfish desires to perpetuate personal ambitions and goals that come at great pain and bad treatment of others. When relationships are broken and not mended, forgiveness has not been extended. With forgiveness there is a change of attitude from selfish desires to a concern of not wanting and being unwilling to achieve goals at the expense of other people. As a process, forgiveness obliges the loss of materials and the personal pain that is caused by a second party.

If one is not careful he may become so attached to the pain of loss of material that so much emphasis is placed there rather than on restoration. The process of forgiveness is the opportunity to rise above what is identified as the norm or expected behavior. With forgiveness this process is not dictated by the standards of the world it is dictated by the words of Jesus through scripture.

Resentment, frustration, pressure and disfellowship will have negative effects on a person if forgiveness is waived for retaliation. Retaliation thrives on "you had it coming to you," "now you know how it feels," "I knew you would get it one day," and "good for you." Forgiveness intervenes and provides assurance over personal loss and hurt and offers assistance to rise above the situation.

Retaliation seeks to tear down at any cost. It leaves a person to suffer when help can be given; it inflicts more pain than that which is already in process. Retaliation is least concerned about fellowship, unity, love and harmony. It waits on time to see a person go under while standing on the sideline cheering as a brother or sister laments in pain.

As the offended person reels in retaliation and waits on time to see the person go under who wronged him, two tragedies are occurring. One is using time as an opportunity to get even. The other is the loss of pleasure and a fuller and meaningful life free of resentment, frustration, pressure and disfellowship void of forgiveness.

The Holy Spirit is available and has great significance for anyone who wants to become subjected to His authority and power without the use of retaliation. The Holy Spirit brings healing and cleansing to an elevation that rules out "my," "I," "me," and "mine," to a love relationship of "Jesus loves me, so shall I love you." Forgiveness is the process through which this can occur.

How unfortunate it is within a body of believers that petty differences, misunderstandings and pains, with the ugliness of no forgiveness, are allowed to manifest themselves. A body divided against itself cannot be a beam of light to lead sinners to Christ. It is apparent then that forgiveness must be the continual mainstream that flows throughout the body to be used on a need basis. Believers within the body are not perfect and as Jesus forgave them of their sins, so should believers continue to forgive each other. For believers, for-giveness must be given for words that are spoken, actions that are seen, thoughts that are repeated, feelings that are expressed, positions that one claimed and the Word that is not read. Believers must readily forgive each other with much love and humbleness. If not, there cannot be peace. Without peace, division manifests itself to cause greater strife and disfellowship. Forgiveness through a process provides the opportunity for spiritual growth and reconciliation for all parties involved to maintain unity.

It is unthinkable that believers cannot forgive one another when they are to be the examples of Christ. But the reality is, people are not without problems and believers in a common body must continue to relate and deal with each other. Disagreement will occur within any body of people because the character of people presents different opinions, conclusions and how specific knowledge should be applied and interpreted.

The disciples of Jesus were filled with different opinions and the application of knowledge that Jesus taught them. Jesus remained loyal to each one with forgiveness as a cornerstone to keep them within His group. Forgiveness keeps a group in tact when Satan says leave; forgiveness allows one to state an opinion even though it may be contrary to everyone else. That one of the 100 must feel needed and wanted by the 99 that provided for individual difference.

If people do not have problems and misunderstandings, there is no need for forgiveness. There are times when a member of the body breaks God's law and the laws of the group. When this occurs, the true test of what the group is about is evident through how it handles the offender. Too often, the experience observed has been to ridicule, embarrass, disfellowship and punish so severely that reconciliation becomes almost impossible for the offender. If Jesus had not extended mercy to the saints of God, salvation would not be a gift; it would be for a price. This does not mean that a body of believers is to condone sin.

If one sins and acknowledges it, then the process of forgiveness should begin. It should not be with an act that says, "Okay everything is all right." Forgiveness offers an opportunity of hope and light for the offended and the offender to process wrong as a sin and process forgiveness as a way to reconcile one back into the body.

In *Webster's New World Concise Dictionary*, forgiveness is defined: "to give up resentment against or the desire to punish; pardon, to overlook an offense, to cancel a debt." Forgiveness recognizes the wrong and rallies to the point of restoration over resentment. It does not look for ways to get even by seeking to make life worse for the offender with self-made tactics of punishment. As a process, forgiveness does not overlook the offense as if it did not hurt or create loss and broken relationships. Forgiveness is an awareness of the pain and hurt that has created broken relationships and rises above all of these to say there is no further charge, there is a clean slate. Welcome back with mercy, come back restored with love and respect. You need not worry about a backlash. You need not concern yourself with "what if?" You have mercy given to me by the father as I give to you.

Forgiveness allows the offended person the opportunity to seek for the restoration and fellowship of a brother or sister condemned by sin to return home. Forgiveness is for the offender to receive and the offended to give. What a gracious act of love there is to be when you are hurt or lose something at the desires of another person, only to say by the process of forgiveness that "you are more important than the lost items or pains received by me." The relationship will not be severed for feelings or losses; it shall manifest itself to an altitude that hurts and pains are not reactivated by contact. The closeness of the relationship opens avenues of prayer and worship with one another with so much power that there is no chance for anything to slip between the relationship.

This allows each person to grow and give worship and prayer to Jesus that is acceptable with mercy.

Forgiveness gives freedom to worship and praise. One cannot be hindered in offering up praises to God when forgiveness has been given. When forgiveness is not given, both parties are bound with no chance for worship and praises to God. Forgiveness must be given to release the offended to continue in worship and allow the offender to join in through reconciliation and mercy to reestablish fellowship to worship. One cannot have fellowship with God unless he has fellowship with his brother. Forgiveness opens the door of fellowship to worship and praise to the Father. Each receives the mercy and grace of God - the offended, because he gave forgiveness and the offender, because he accepted forgiveness without restrictions. These two become united to appeal to the lost world that Jesus died for us and His forgiveness is available for restoration with all that will accept it. A unit is not divided against itself. It is strong in power and has a force that is attractive to those displaced in drugs, alcohol, starvation, low self-esteem and crime. The attraction remains in the words, "You are forgiven."

CHAPTER 2

Forgiving Yourself

People are living in complex situations and have sentenced themselves not being worthy of life because of terrible deeds they have committed. Some people refuse to believe that they can have relationships based on admiration and respect, overshadowed with forgiveness. The words are repeated, "Nobody cares and I do not either." Many people have made mistakes and live to regret them. They torture themselves over events that occurred years earlier and refuse to say, "I made a mistake. I cannot redo it. I cannot change the circumstances under which they occurred. If I am going to get anywhere in my life, or move on, I must accept the blame and forgive myself."

This process provides a relationship with Christ so that God forgives the sins of a sinner with a repentant heart. An allegiance is made that God forgives and to forgive oneself is to believe and accept forgiveness. A person is under bondage when personal forgiveness is not accepted. This burden is too excessive to carry and nothing that people make, say or do can rid the mind to have inner peace. There is nothing available for obtaining except the process of forgiveness. Forgiveness releases the burden, pain and guilt to Jesus. He takes the burden, cleanses the mind and allows us to go on with life even when there is punishment by man. In the middle of personal storms, peace, wonderful peace, can be bestowed. Barney Elliott Warren's song, "Peace" states,

"Sweet peace is flowing, peace that will abide
Peace e'er increasing, Jesus will provide;

Peace like a river in the time of drought,
Flowing forever from the sunny mouth.
Sweet peace in Jesus never can be told.
Oh, it is glorious, better far than gold.
Showers are falling all around me here.
Peace that is amazing, desert hearts to cheer."[3]

To have peace one must seek God's forgiveness, confess sins and ask for forgiveness. Upon receiving it, give thanks and praise to Jesus Christ. To know and to be relieved of all the hurt, agony and pain that come with forgiveness will bring peace. What sweeter word can an individual have than the word forgiveness? It lifts the load of guilt and provides pardon under the blood of Jesus. Forgiveness gives security through the love Christ has for a man. Christ substituted Himself through pain and death so that individual redemption may be accomplished. In his book, Morning and Evening, Charles Spurgeon states, "When I think of how great my sins were, how dear were the precious drops which cleansed me from them and the gracious act which sealed my pardon, I am filled with wondering, worshiping affection. I bow before the throne which absorbs me. I clasp the cross which delivers me. I serve the Incarnate God through which I am a pardoned soul."[4] There is joy of the soul that accepts the forgiveness, which is given by God, and there is the door that becomes available for the greatest relationship known to man.

If one is to grow into a fuller relationship with Christ, there must be self-examination. This must be done with the belief that Jesus is available and that there is a need to get rid of the bondage that prevents freedom of worship. Too often a person cannot look beyond personal failures to feel the need for the acceptance of forgiveness. Or, there may be severe hurt and loss to one that was close at one time.

Rather than deal with the situation to reestablish the relationship, one may opt to leave things as they are.

Self-pity may surface to a point that one begins to feel unworthy of the wrong committed and cannot rise above the act to thrive on the process of forgiveness. In Matthew 27, 3-5 it states: "Then Judas, which had betrayed him, when he saw that he was condemned, repented himself, and brought again the thirty pieces of silver to the chief priests and elders, Saying, I have sinned in that I have betrayed the innocent blood. And they said, What is that to us? see thou to that. And he cast down the pieces of silver in the temple, and departed, and went and hanged himself."[2] Judas betrayed Jesus by turning against Him and conspiring with Jesus' enemies. And when the enemies of Jesus condemned Him, Judas took a different position. He had a sense of guilt that allowed him to go back to the elders and chief priests to return the silver which he could not keep. The silver was no longer of value because Judas recognized a broken relationship that was not his to claim. Judas acknow-ledged the problem by saying, "I have sinned. Why have I sinned? Because I have betrayed innocent blood." He is straight forth with the wrong committed, the way it was committed and accepted the personal acts of having sinned. It was at this point that Judas could have intervened with himself and said, "Master! I am sorry, please forgive me." Judas had been with Jesus and knew how He worked and forgave men and women of their sins. But the people who used him no longer had use of him, and he stood alone. This was the very time that Jesus made himself available to the outcast and hurting.

It is as if the world which had a happy time with Judas said, "No more. I am happy without you." Note the words were not a part of the conversation when Judas presented himself to be a player with those to destroy Jesus. A goal was set, an act was committed and the desired results were accomplished. But they were not what Judas wanted. He was not satisfied and returned the money and told why he was doing so. Judas was apparently at a low point in his life. Could he have said, "Woe is me! I did wrong to someone who did not deserve it. What did I do? Why?"

Judas turned the pain, hurt and loss within himself and left it there. The load was too heavy for him to carry. The pain was too great for his body and mind to handle and he could not come up with a solution to rectify the problem. The process of forgiveness was available to release him of all the pain and hurt. This process would have identified the problem and not held it to remind him of the wrong done to Jesus. Forgiveness was available to Judas to reject or accept. But because he was so involved over his mistake, he could not forgive himself and the only way out was to hang himself. Rejection of one's self leaves little opportunity for restoration. One must accept the blame of committing wrong, yet not allow the wrong to dictate the future.

Judas' conscience was evident to him. He sold the Master for a small sum thinking that he would have inner peace. When one commits wrongs and seeks to change it without mercy and grace by the offended person, often the results are fatal. Judas did not reach for mercy. He sought relief within his power and thought that his sins were greater than forgiveness.

There is no substitute that a person may offer to replace forgiveness. The price is too high, the load is too heavy and the disfellowship is too great for an unpardoned soul to seek relief by other means rather than through the one right way of forgiveness.

One must also humble himself to a point of saying, "I am wrong and I must keep assistance beyond what I am able to give." When one becomes humble, the opportunity for shortcoming becomes more pronounced and the stage is established for modesty. As one becomes keenly aware of who and what he is, there is the greater chance for the acceptance of forgiveness. Yet, with a forgiving Savior and forgiving people, the offender must accept it with grace through an element of mercy.

A man with a hard heart, tough ego and with strong determination to destroy others is set forth in this motion because he has not forgiven himself for his actions. One cannot move any further in life than that which he has within himself. If nothing is there to guide and discipline his nature and relationship with other people, he needs to recognize and accept the process of forgiveness.

Forgiveness gives such a person the recognition of worth and pronounces him fit for values beyond things and ideas. As forgiveness is extended, it must be accepted through the love which Jesus gave for all men when He said, "It is finished." One cannot redo that which has ended. The only remaining feature is the need for personal salvation with a loving and caring Savior. When one accepts the forgiveness given by the Savior he becomes a partner in love, knowing that mercy is the payment for the end product. "Yet but for the mercy of God, there go I." Mercy intervened to give a chance when none was deserved. Mercy opened the door to challenge any who would say, "I deserve this. This is mine because of the debt I paid." Jesus is the focus and as He forgave, so must a person forgive himself.

To forgive one's self is to be restored to the majesty and power of meaningful relationships that are built on forgiveness as a way out without trying to repay or destroy a life. The greatest thing a person may have for himself or herself is the process of forgiveness. Through this there is no cost to charge, no debt to pay, no future to hide from and no people to dishonor. Just the acceptance, "I am forgiven."

CHAPTER 3

Forgiving Others

To forgive others is to be forgiven by the heavenly Father. To not forgive others is to not be forgiven by the heavenly Father. Matthew 6:14-15 reads: "For if ye forgive men their trespasses your heavenly Father will also forgive you: But if ye forgive not men their trespasses, neither will your Father forgive your trespasses."[2] To deny forgiveness is to deny that the gift of forgiveness exists in God through Christ. One must be forgiven as he seeks forgiveness. This process is a gift that must be given liberally without restrictions.

Man's relationships with one another are the opportunities to be kind and tenderhearted. This should outweigh the meanness and cruelty toward another. Praying for those who persecute you is a reminder of the process that activates forgiveness with compassion. How would one feel if he was in the other person's shoes? It may be easier to try to do harm and be judgmental of every act committed toward oneself, but the rewards are much greater when the conflicts are resolved and people continue with their lives free in the process of forgiveness.

Forgiving others should be a visible trademark of the local church. Every person that is a part of the fellowship has had the experience of forgiveness and the release of burdens attached with heavy loads.[5]

In the process of forgiving, it is important for the person extending forgiveness not to expect reciprocation. Forgiveness is the recognition of personal loss, hurt and no respect for the privacy and materials of another person. It takes under consideration that pride, character, recognition, peers and non-peers are less important and must be vacated to extend forgiveness. Forgiveness recognizes personal anger, frustration, the thought of getting even and the need to be reimbursed for loss, and rightly so. Forgiveness goes beyond all these and states in spite of loss, character, anger and frustration, that these processes are important and essential. When forgiveness is extended, there is no doubt that it is sincere even though unwarranted.

There must be some understanding of the person without trying to get even. Understanding allows one to not become obsessed with the thought of being hurt. Nor does it provide all the answers to why one would offend another. The real purpose of understanding is to help one see the difference between what the sinner did and who the sinner is and recognize wrong for what it is. Recognize the person for the wrong committed and rise above the place of bitterness and hatred to a place of love. Love for another person compels the offended to reach out and seeks to reestablish ties above willful, wrong acts.

To love another is to trust you are being loved by the Master. As the Master loved so must the offended person love. To love and care for someone when things are going good is easy. The real person surfaces when that which is loved is hurt, abused or destroyed by an offender. Should one expect to forgive another in these situations? The answer is yes. With the help of the Master this can be achieved.

Forgiving others brings to focus that another has merit and value above the wrong deeds committed. To not acknowledge a person as being important enough to warrant love and forgiveness, relationships cannot be mended for the future. As painful as it is, relationships must be more important than things and the acts committed to or upon another must be placed at a level with love perpetuated with forgiveness. One cannot forgive nothing, nor can one forgive things. It is people that must be forgiven. As Christ died on the cross, His highest aim was to establish a process by which man would have a personal relationship with the Father. How was this to be accomplished? There would have to be a way of removing debt, penalty or cost. Jesus said, "Father forgive." In the forgiving process there is no debt or cost, only freedom to the offender.

To forgive another does not allow for one to be ignored or denied the opportunity to be the best that he can become. Forgiveness gives the opportunity to be the best that he can become. Forgiveness gives the opportunity to become that which according to the law is impossible. Forgiving others is the responsibility and knowledge of having accepted forgiveness. It is not with compassion that a person is considered to be worthless and not wanted. Compassion allows one to help or assist another to be better or the opportunity to get better.

All have come short of the glory of God, the offended and the offender. Therefore, those within the Church and those outside of the Church have the responsibility of saying thanks for having mercy with forgiveness. This process when completed in one situation may need to resurface to be given in a different situation. Daily, people need to be forgiven. Imperfect people will continue to make mistakes that warrant forgiveness. Living within a society allows people to see wrong deeds done to others as well as themselves. There must be, and needs to be, a separation of the deeds from the person. When this is done people will be seen for what they may become rather than for what they are.

Jesus saw man in sin and offered a plan for what he may become. When forgiveness is given, the opportunity for growth is high. No low achievers, only high ones. To see people as they are through the hurt, loss and frustration opens the door with the words, "You are forgiven by me". Forgiveness gives the opportunity to love when hate is expected, to care when pains have been experienced, to open the door when locks are expected to be found, to extend a hand when one is expected to be withdrawn, to release when pain says keep it and wait for the time to say it's your turn now. It is better to be a carrier of a boat with love, concern and care heightened with forgiveness than to be a ship of hate, malice and grudges. When the tide of life moves forward, the boat will float in the ocean while the ship will sink in the smallest wave.

Forgiveness excludes itself from the law. The law is there to punish and forgiveness is there for freedom. The law sets restraints. Forgiveness restores broken relationships and offers hope that could be lost forever. Walls come down that one in his own power perceives never to be possible. Forgiveness begins with a process and ends with a miracle. It is not an equation that can be written and followed. It is not reaction to action. It is to be built on the merit of another through bitterness, tears and denial of self. It is redemption of a lost soul at the cliff of a mountain leaning to fall over, only to have a net of love for a rescue saying you shall not go at my loss or pain. You shall gain a place of self-esteem not expected. As one stands and is about to go over the cliff, the very person that was harmed offers hands and says, "Give up your pain for my mercy of forgiveness."

As the two walk from the edge of the cliff hand in hand, streams and rivers of tests must be crossed to see if there is an act of forgiveness or a process. In the rivers and streams the act will save one but in the process two will be saved. It has been stated that it is not an easy road. Let's not pretend that it is. It is a hard and dangerous road that life presents when one does harm to those that are loved and appreciated. The windows of opportunities for forgiveness are not for use when things are going good. It is only useful when things are going bad. Forgiveness is of no pleasure when things are good. It has no value without crisis. It can only be granted at the height of the greatest hurt, the deepest pain and the greatest loss. Forgiveness as a process of acceptance opens a door and says, walk with me in a relationship with no return favors, just acceptance of what is on the table. Mercy, love and forgiveness are needed because this is what the Master gave to the world.

This process takes time, it cannot be hurried, but it must be achieved. There is no extension on time. Time locks all of us in to sequences of events and conditions. The use of it sets into motion how we feel about others and the price to be paid for such feelings.

A young lady revealed that she was about to commit murder against someone who did wrong unjustly and she perceived that she had enough and this was her only way out of the situation. As she was in motion to complete the act, the telephone rang. She stopped to answer only to hear a voice on the other end of the line over a thousand miles away say, "Do not do it." The right call, the right place, the right time prevented two lives from being destroyed. Today this lady speaks the words, "I have no malice in my heart. I feel no pain. I have forgiven this person because the Lord has forgiven me of my sins. And Glory, Hallelujah, I am free!"

The process of forgiving others allows praise and freedom of worship with prayer and thanksgiving. This same lady now claims salvation for all her children because of the joy that is experienced by her through the power of forgiveness. The process of forgiveness entitles one to say, "I am free". It releases burdens and brings grace and mercy from Jesus, which is in turn given to another person. The process does not stop; it cannot offer to be turned away at the expense of selfish desires. One is freed from one experience to be prepared for another as the opportunity presents itself. How many times shall forgiveness be given during the life of a person? It shall be given as often as it is needed. Forgiveness exceeds boundary lines of states and countries; it does not restrict itself to families. It goes to those whose names were heard without ever meeting them. It crosses battlefields of wars and rage from a bullet of death to a hug of, "I am sorry, please forgive me."

In our society today, there are too many teen killings because they have denied the process of forgiveness and tried to conclude their problems with guns, gangs, alcohol and the selfish desire to get even. When one opts to get even, it takes less than 10 seconds to destroy a life and be in bondage for life. This process releases tension without guns and sets in motion shared relationships at early ages that bind and hold strong ties between young people.

When resentment and undisciplined children are allowed to roam at will, there is a price to be paid and all too often it is at the expense of the life of another. There are no perfect parents, only forgiving ones. There are no perfect children, only good children that have experienced the process of forgiveness, while those identified as bad need to experience the process of forgiveness. To forgive another person is real, with dynamic power. To offer forgiveness, one must have experienced it. To receive forgiveness, one must have need of it. To deny forgiveness, one must not appreciate it.

People do cruel things to take advantage of situations that are not limited to lying, stealing or admitting to errors. Some are just plain meanness and selfishness. But, to the offended, there must remain a ray of hope and a strain on raw nerves to offer forgiveness to others rather than trample under their feet to be lost forever in the arena of time.

CHAPTER 4

Profess Forgiveness in Theory by Abandoning it in Practice

One of the greatest barriers in not forgiving is when one pretends that everything is alright when it is not. When a person does not own up to the pains of loss and the frustration associated with them, forgiveness cannot be given. Admit you hurt me! You took what was mine! You cannot repay! Even if you had money, it cannot pay for my pain!

The tragedy of this is that people try to skip this process and go to the act of forgiving. How can one forgive without knowing the conditions under which it should be given and the elements of loss that are accepted to extend forgiveness?

To deny hurt and loss is to deny forgiveness. Forgiveness in theory is correct and has been tested and experienced to know that it is the right thing to do. Jesus is our example with perfection.[6] Forgiveness must be done with sincerity and without any stumbling blocks to fall back upon. There is no excuse to say I forgive then recreate barriers of extending forgiveness. Having gone through the recognition of all to be in fellowship with another is worth more than professing forgiveness.

It is a phony person that states the act of forgiveness and abandons it in practice. Jesus forgave in theory and practiced it. He did not have to do it. He went beyond feelings, holding grudges or pointing to the problem. He activated the theory and did not abandon the practice of forgiveness. What joy, peace and fellowship one can have with himself if forgiveness is professed in theory and not abandoned in practice.

What pain, hurt and disfellowship one can have with himself if forgiveness is professed in theory and abandoned in practice. One cannot be phony in the process of forgiveness simply because there is no ray of hope for restoration of the two parties. A phony person is one that is false, a fake and not genuine in what is said or done. Jesus paid a high price for forgiveness to have it locked in the mind of one who chooses not to be real.

Forgiveness is an act of freedom and must remain so because of its worth and value of reconciliation. The process cannot be forced or accomplished by tact, manipulation or gifts. It must not be attempted under the stress of a crowd to pressure one to say that which is not sincere. It is not a duty to be used at will. It is the upper level of core and concern which reaches beyond personal desire or accomplishments to offer freedom though undeserved.

A wife or husband that needs forgiveness from their spouse must keep in mind that forgiveness is not designed for reminders and control. Nothing is worse than to be told that you are forgiven and then be nagged for what was done. How can one feel a sense of relief when the opportunity is not given for freedom? Through the process of forgiveness there is no power of love when one is plagued with reruns of all the things from the past. The person that is running the reruns is not free and cannot free the offender.

It is better for both persons to gain victory for each other with honesty than with a whip. A whip leaves its mark every time it is used. It is used to cause pain and leave scars. A person that gives scars has not forgiven and cannot be forgiven. To say to another that you are forgiven and bind the person in bondage is without merit and care.

Ephesians 4:29 reads: "Let no corrupt communication proceed out of your mouth, but that which is good to the use of edifying, that it may minister grace unto the hearers."[2] Degrading a person through words does not help anyone, nor does it offer solutions to problems. The best news an offender can hear is that which is said with edification and grace.

In Ephesians 4:31 and 32, note these words: "Let all bitterness, and wrath, and anger, and clamor, and evil speaking, be put away from you, with all malice. And be ye kind one to another, tenderhearted, forgiving one another, even as God for Christ's sake hath forgiven you."[2] It is important that the offended person acknowledge the offender, without bitterness and anger. There cannot be evil speaking to the offender or to others about the offender. These cannot be part of the process of forgiving. When one is overwhelmed with bitterness, malice, evil words, wrath and anger, there is room for forgiveness to be held and appreciated. This is forgiveness in theory while abandoning it in practice. The theory of forgiveness does not help anyone and cannot be used to deliver a person out of a pit of shame and failures to a light of inspiration and hope. What a better society of people we would have if kindness was placed in action rather than a word with no meaning. Kindness must be given from one to another to have an in-road to the hearts of men to activate forgiveness. A tenderhearted person is touched with compassion for another because of forgiveness given by God. All have come short of the glory of God and need forgiveness. As God offered forgiveness to man so must all offer forgiveness to one another.

Acts are steps toward the process of forgiveness. It is the beginning of an end. It does not consider the occurrence of what one may become, it only identifies with self. It does not seek to be reconciled; its only interest is "me", "I", and "mine". The process of forgiveness challenges one to interact for the best interest of the offender at the loss of the offended.

Theory in forgiveness has merit because it has been proven and withstood the test of time. The practice of forgiveness offers many challenges and opens doors to reconciliation.

One who forgives in theory and abandons it in practice is hypocritical and his words have no value. There cannot be room for the experience of saying, "I am sorry, please forgive me" when one is not honest. One who has been hurt will not go any further in life than the theory that is believed in. Forgiveness shadows theory and says let's do it with practice. Practice allows one to build on trust and confidence. Practice recognizes the need to displace any opportunity to prove what is right or what is wrong. There is a new beginning when two people offer each other the symbol of opportunity to continue the practice of forgiveness. One that has the experience of practice may grow to become a person of value rather than one that is a phony.

Forgiveness through a process gives the offender an opportunity to see events as they are and to analyze the loss, pain or frustration created by the offender. The pain and frustration may not be personal; it could be displaced to someone closely associated as a family member or friend. But, the pain can be just as severe. When the offended person realizes that an act has been made that causes pain, resentment and losses, the choice of holding a grudge may become a factor that initiates getting back at any cost, or taking another way out. One must realize the lost and inner feelings as they are and seek to maintain a good relationship. In the process of forgiveness, a person must know the pain, who caused it, the extent of the damage and then generate a positive attitude toward the offender without malice. To do this a recognition must be made of the anger for the offended act and realize that hurt may not go away for awhile, but the decision for forgiveness must supersede every emotion not to forgive. There must be a closed door to personal pride, release of personal rights and the fear of being wrong again. An honest forthright reality of all the negatives against forgiveness must be considered in terms of one's relationship with God, the offender and oneself. The need to get back or get even cannot be a decision for one who is offended. A child may state that he loves and has forgiven a mother on alcohol, or a father on drugs. Simply stating that one is forgiven is not enough. There must be an effort for reconciliation and freedom through fellowship. Fellowship allows people to interact with each other. It becomes aware of weakness and disagreement. It tests the patience of one to see if fellowship is bound by a process above hurt and shame.

When one has served time for a crime he did not commit, where does forgiveness begin? Is it within oneself to experience relief from the desire to get back everything lost during the time spent in prison? There must be a commitment that one will deal with self for the right answers. To be expected to say all is well is easy, but it may not be the correct thing to say because it is not of the heart. There have been people who have criticized others because of their failure to express forgiveness. There is no pain more unbearable than to say in an act that all is forgiven when it is not. Who has the right to torment another person, shame, kill, mistreat or lie against another, and then expect the offended to forget and say let's move on with our lives? No human has the right to expect another person to do this. Forgiveness cuts to the core of pain and grief. How can one be expected to live to love another who caused such misery? The mind may protest this as a cowardly act. Yet, the heart must resist because forgiving is the only way we have fairness in our unfair world.

It is love's unexpected revolution against unfair pain, and it alone offers strong hope for healing the hurts we so unfairly feel.[7] To feel pain that hurts to the heart and be agitated by an act of forgiveness is not enough. Guilty! Guilty! must come the verdict of hurt and pain. Only to be released by the Master's pleas, "Forgive those who trespass against you." The process of forgiveness must be the ultimate goal of accomplishment of the offended to rise above theory, but never beyond practice.

CHAPTER 5

Forgiveness is Not Perfection

Forgiveness does not present one with the crown of great success, nor does it place one in the elite society within the Church or the world. It humbles one to look within himself for what he truly is before God and man.

To forgive does not bring honor. It does not negate a continuous flow of being forgiven and continually extending the process which is needed daily by the forgiven. Forgiving is the joy of restoring fellowship with another person. It is not designed for one's pleasure of being made to feel that a certain level of utopia has been achieved. The process of forgiveness is not for perfection. It is for the act or acts committed by an individual in a given situation. Through the process one may learn how vulnerable he is when someone does wrong to him. It is for the person extending forgiveness to release hate to obtain joy, to release bitterness for sweetness of words, to release anger for compassion, to release pain for healing, to release blame for responsibility, to release the unaccepted to acceptance, to release partiality for wholeness, to release self-pity and pride to freedom and glory, and to release one in bondage with Satan to freedom with Chirst.[8]

The personal satisfaction given in forgiveness releases one from the perplexity of being condemned and magnifies one with a stronger relationship with Christ and with himself.

One who is in a state of perfection does not need to achieve, he has achieved. In St. John 8:1-11, Jesus was standing with the woman caught in adultery that was brought to Him by the scribes and Pharisees. They stated the law of

Moses and the consequences given by the law. Determined to carry out the law to the fullest extent, these men had no compassion. Is it not strange that the person the lady was with was not also brought before the mob? Why? Could it have been to cover up personal acts that they were guilty of doing? Jesus, being the wise Father that He was, stooped and began to write in the sand with His finger. Those who being perfect in condemning saw themselves when Jesus made the statement, "He that is without sin among you, let him first cast a stone at her."[2] Note that each person left and Jesus asked the question to the woman, "Woman, where are those thine accusers? Hath no man condemned thee? She said, No man, Lord. And Jesus said unto her, Neither do I condemn thee: go, and sin no more."[2] Forgiveness was given without the word "forgive" being stated. The process by which Jesus went through to indicate forgiveness released the woman to express herself as a lady and remind others that no one is perfect in sin or out of sin.

He that is without sin and does not need the forgiveness of the Father cast the first stone. All have come short of the blessings of the Father. Only with "grace" can one call on Him to be reminded that forgiving is not perfection. It is the opportunity to let go of personal demands, disgust and egos. It allows one to be in fellowship through Jesus and with an offender. Forgiveness lets go and does not live in the past, nor does it attach the pain and hurt to relive the experience caused by the offender of the pain.

How sad it is when the offended places himself above the offender by outlining the procedure for forgiveness to be acceptable to him. One would seem to say, in my perfection to have the chance to get you (the offender) right; I'll use you as an example of what forgiveness is. Note however, that this is not a time for the offended to elevate himself to set standards. It is the opportunity to become humble by those processes already in place by Jesus. It is letting go of pain to get release and moving toward perfection without ever reaching it. It is a way of pressing over the wrong committed and the opportunity to get rid of the notion to become elevated to a place of having achieved perfection.

Life does not present perfect solutions or perfect problems for imperfect people. Thus, they are faced with the repeated experience that allows for growth and spiritual maturity in Jesus. In Philippians 3:12-14, Paul states, "Not as though I had already attained, either were already perfect: but I follow after, if that I may apprehend that for which also I am apprehended of Christ Jesus. Brethren, I count not myself to have apprehended: but this one thing I do, forgetting those things which are behind, and reaching forth unto those things which are before, I press toward the mark for the prize of the high calling of God in Christ Jesus."[2]

One cannot be locked into the past to experience giving or receiving forgiveness. This act prevents the process from being activated and everyone loses. Defining the problem to a time and place and holding one there is in effect denying that forgiveness works. To recognize the events and know the pain was severe does not give one the chance to say, here I stand and I change not. The inner character of one must realize that with forgiveness there is no attainment, just forgetting the past which binds and holds one back from moving forward in love. The future is open for reconciliation under the power of Jesus as one presses to the calling of Christ Jesus.

Too often there may be a feeling of great accomplishment when one has forgiven another. In this process one may become sidetracked into being superior over the offender. This does not help because forgiveness does not place burdens or obligations upon the offender. It places opportunity for the offender to accept the mercy plea and seek to bind it with the forgiveness which comes from the Master.

One cannot afford to rate himself when extending forgiveness to another. It is not a game of point. It is the chance for the offended to look within himself and see himself as what he could be in a relationship built on love. Being good is not the answer for extending forgiveness. Goodness is not a formula that one can use to heighten personal character. A person cannot ride on the waves of emotion to have pity and sorrow for an offender. There must be a personal examination to dethrone goodness, character and any other thing that may cause one to feel better than the offender.

For the forgiving to extend forgiveness, a process must be examined, accepted and realized that love has an important role in the process. Forgiveness should not be testified as a great achievement. It is to be claimed as power of Christ Jesus and it should be given as a gift of mercy because of what Christ paid for all. If not for the grace of God, each person would be in a fix if punishment was the recipient. Only through the grace of God is man forgiven. Only by continuing the process of forgiveness with those that are offenders that one may say, I am forgiven.

There will not be a plaque for the wall, or clapping in a special celebration. It will only be Jesus at the experience to call attention to the process as you have forgiven; you are also forgiven by the Father. No honor may be given, no praise may be bestowed, yet the greatest claim one may take hold of is that Jesus knows man is not perfect, only forgiven.

Perfection is the desired result for one to achieve. One may set a goal to reach perfection, but the reality is that man has flaws and this will continue to be so. Flaws did not alter Jesus' love for a person. He saved people with flaws to be used by Him for His glory.

Perfection, if possible, gives one the pride of disbelief that he does not need anything or anyone. It sets one apart from all others. It provides one with the feeling that everything said is correct and everything accomplished is without question. This is a downfall of one's mind and attitude, and the only direction that one may be headed is down.

Perfection is of the Lord. No sin did He do, no hatred did He have. His perfection was in love for man. His pain for man was death on the cross. A perfect Jesus for an imperfect man. Jesus did not offer man perfection. He only provided forgiveness for sin as a way of restoration to the Father.

As man continues to offer forgiveness, there cannot be a claim for perfection. "All have come short." This is enough said to call attention that as men relate to each other, there will always be a need for the process of forgiveness to continue. As great a process as forgiveness is for the offended and offender, perfection does not end at the process of forgiveness. Nor does it begin with pain of the offender. Perfection cannot be a solution for forgiveness. Forgiveness is not an indication of how perfect one is. It is an opportunity for one to continue to press on toward the prize of Jesus.

CHAPTER 6

The Pain of Forgiving

Forgiveness is associated with hurt and frustration. The process of forgiving does not exit the hurt nor does it open itself to be relieved of suffering. As one suffers loss from another, the question comes to mind: Why forgive with the pain I am in, or have experienced since the process will cause more pain? How unbearable is pain when the words remind us, "I will not put more on you than you can bear." Is the pain of forgiveness greater than the fellowship of Jesus? Is it worth disfellowship with Jesus and man not to forgive another because of pain involved in the process?

As one extends forgiveness to another who is not repentant or shows no cause that he may ever be repentant for acts committed, a process of forgiveness is essential to deal with a harsh enemy. The process has within it a miracle of healing that is comfort beyond the pain of one who does not accept responsibility for personal actions nor the consequences imposed on another.

To extend forgiveness when it is refused by the offender is painful for the giver. Yet, the process is so important to the offended person that nothing must be allowed to stop it. Forgiveness begins with Jesus and one must be in fellowship with him for the process to be completed. The offended person, as hard as it may seem, must remain prepared to forgive with reconciliation as the main goal.

Often the expression, "forgive and forget", has caused many problems for the offended person. To forgive is not to forget. This may be because of the severity of the offense.

The mind has the ability to keep facts and events, yet the person becomes bound to the principle: I will not bring up the event to you, I will not bring it up to others, and I will not bring it up to myself. The wrong committed is a dead issue. The process is completed.

When one process of forgiveness is completed, other opportunities present themselves to activate it again. One process of forgiveness does not filter one pain in another situation. Pain comes physically, mentally, socially and spiritually. The one thing man tries to do in all of his experiences is to avoid pain. Pain hurts to the core of life itself. So much so that rather than face it, many people have taken their lives. Oh, for the sweetness of life, how happy and enjoyable it would be if there was no pain. Pain humbles the proud, the rich, the famous, the educated and even the unrepentant person. Pain brings one to a state of reality. For each person, no matter what his or her circumstances, pain has the power to heighten their character or cause it to default.

Forgiveness is a process that is complex and painful with hurt, loss and wrongdoing of another's welfare. It is a journey of processes that require undertaking one at a time. Each process may, and can be, very painful and difficult. It is often not accomplished with leaps and bounds, but by a careful, thoughtful process with deep reflection. Forgiveness can be given with no restrictions, even with pain if taken one step at a time. It is important to remember that no one ever really forgives another, except he bears the penalty of the other's sin against him. And with this process there will be pain.

Pain is real and no one is allowed to escape it. Pain hurts; it affects one externally and internally. Pain presents the question, why me. And at a point in one's life there may be an attempt to stop pain at all cost. This becomes dangerous for the offended and the offender. Pain can cause so much hurt that it eats away at the healing process of forgiveness.

Pain comes in all kinds of situations. It may be the loss of a job, or overlooked when there is a promotion. A drunken mother or father may cause pain. The use of drugs by children or adults, the death of a love one, divorce, being lied on, deception by a friend, all of these and more may create pain. People cause pain and the effect of it is real. Is there an escape from it? Is it always a target for a specific person, or does it just happen?

Many times people hurt themselves through their own actions and shortcomings. They allow themselves to be used and abused without trying to resolve issues. A stormy marriage where the husband is an abuser can be more painful when the wife allows herself to be continually abused. Which is better, stay and be abused or leave with less pain? People will hurt no matter what course of action they take. Life does not take on being fair. Pain is unfair when people do not deserve it or when it is not necessary. But, the reality is that people intend to hurt. Their goal is to destroy and cause great damage. At other times a person's intention may be interpreted to be bad when it was for good. Yet pain can be the end result.

Pain can cause people to fight back because the offender hurt them when there was no need for it. Sometimes people hurt because of their pain or the pain they feel for another close to them. In 2nd Samuel, Chapter 13, Absalom's sister Tamar was raped by Amnon. When Absalom heard what his brother did to his sister he was angry. The anger grew and revenge set in to get even. Two years passed and revenge sought for an opportunity to get even. When the opportunity presented itself, Absalom had his servant kill Amnon for raping his sister. The tragedy here is that Amnon raped his sister and caused great pain for Tamar because of the shame. And for Absalom there was great pain because of humiliation, harm and the ruined life of his sister. Here a brother chose to satisfy his lust at the expense of his sister and then hate her for what he did. The other brother, Absalom, hated with duration just to get even for the act and pain of his sister. Her pain in effect became his pain and her shame was in effect his shame. And the only way, as Absalom saw it, was to kill his brother for this unwarranted pain.

When a person is hurt and does not deal with it in an honest way, then seeks to justify getting even by killing, nobody wins. The pain started out with Amnon and Tamar, spread to Absalom, and because Absalom allowed hatred to set in, he had his brother killed. Amnon should have been disciplined by his father, David, for his act. And Amnon should have been punished to a point that his father would let all others know this would not be tolerated in his household. Here was pain that was experienced by many and no forgiveness was given.

Let's look at Absalom. Did he have the right to be angry at what happened to his sister? He had the right to be angry with his brother and there was no denying the fact that a terrible thing was done to Tamar. It would have been fair, right and just for Absalom to approach his brother and seek to get some resolution for the act. But when that which is not fair occurs and acts of hatred follow to rectify fairness, there can only be more trouble. That which is fair, right and just may not get its due reward. Sometimes fairness, righteousness and that which is just receive punishment. And punishment creates more punishment until the chain is broken with forgiveness. Amnon did not deserve to be killed; Tamar did not deserve to be raped, but they occurred. What now? No one should be hated. Hatred destroyed two people, the one to whom hatred was given and the person who was giving hatred. An eye for an eye, where will it stop? Every human soul has the right to be free from hate and claim a rightful inheritance through the process of forgiveness. This process must be granted to the one that does harm to those we love so dearly.

The process of forgiveness does not play around with the deep wounds caused by pain. Often pain is where it should not be. And the one who is the recipient of it must know and feel it as an opportunity to forgive deep hurts. One must evaluate the facts, as they are, being aware that conditions cannot be changed. Attitudes can be changed and they may come from the offended person. The cry, "it hurts so badly" is a far cry from the pains that can last a lifetime without forgiveness.

There is slow death created when one allows one's self to hate. Hate takes control of the mind and emotions and thrives on the offender getting his due reward. Hate may become so violent that one may lose any feeling or disregard for the loss of a life. Hate causes more pain of troubles and disappointment. Hate may continue uncontrolled by selfish passion and bad motives. Hatred grows beyond the circumstances that caused it to surface and create additional pain for the hater, the person being hated and many times innocent victims that were not involved in any of the acts.

When hate is active, the pain of forgiveness is dormant. A person must acknowledge that he feels betrayed, ridiculed, hurt and wounded by the acts or act of the offender. This is a positive move in the right direction to realize the pain personally felt and the hurt and loss which goes with it. With the loss and pain, one must see the offender as a person that is in need of being forgiven along with the continued pain that forgiveness brings. Forgiveness must be the process by which one involves himself to the end. There cannot be toleration of the person as the offender because of the desire to prevent additional pain. Forgiveness must be the way to grind away at the hurt and agony one may experience. It provides a way out of constant pain, hatred and the will to get back at the person. Forgiveness sets in motion the offended person to reach out and say, "With the pain I have already experienced, and with the pain I now feel, I release myself and you for a renewed fellowship". This fellowship shall restore lives. It allows the offender that accepts forgiveness and the offended that gives it away to move forward.

Forgiveness only seeks an opportunity for a beginning. With it, hurt no longer becomes a priority for revenge, but an opportunity for restoration. Forgiveness opens a door of respect for an offender and it allows his freedom to grow without restraints. With forgiveness there is a healing process that will not allow bitterness, malice and control to be the main focus for holding a person. With pain, there can and must be forgiveness. It must be as one is; there cannot be a created change or a molding of a person to extend forgiveness. Forgiveness must be given to be totally accepted or rejected. Even with pain there cannot be any pre-existing or pro-existing conditions for it to work.

Jesus' forgiveness of men caused great pain, agony and finally death. His focus was not on his condition, but the forgiveness given for the world for the redemption of sin. When a person experiences pain at the cost of another, forgiveness gives freedom from this condition to build a renewed relationship. Relationships have to be built on trust and love. When this fails, forgiveness is offered against all claims against all pains and against all hurts. Thus, forgiveness cannot be a created act for the moment. It must be from the heart. It must be wrapped in boldness and open for all to see. The wrong received must be visible to the heart. It cannot be covered as if it did not occur. If there is no pain, then there is no need for forgiveness. One must have freedom from the pain that he gave and one must have freedom from the pain that he received.[7]

Oh, for the pain that broke my heart. How could I this pain deny? How can I refuse to say the pain and hurt affected me? Am I to go on and not see the trouble you cause me, or grant you freedom while I ponder the reason? My mind does not allow it to be. My heart, though broken, is not shattered by the lingering thought; get even, no matter what it takes. I'll run to the Master for my sake, to hear His call and plea for me. Never fret my child; I'll take care of thee. Forgiveness is freedom and liberty. So run with pain hard and strong. You shall have the victory accompanied by me.

Sin may be the cause, but forgiveness can be the cure.

CHAPTER 7

Forgiving with the Love of Jesus

"Hatred stirreth up strifes: but love covereth all sins"[2], Proverbs 10:12. "A new commandment I give unto you, That ye love one another; as I have loved you, that ye also love one another"[2], St. John 13:34. "But I say unto you which hear, Love your enemies, do good to them which hate you, Bless them that curse you, and pray for them which despitefully use you"[2], St. Luke 6:27-28.

Jesus had so much love for the world that He died for it. And on the cross He extended forgiveness to those responsible for His suffering. Jesus is love. He practiced it and transformed the lives of men by the love He demonstrated and practiced with those in and out of His presence. To ask the Father to forgive His enemies in the midst of physical pain is the character of Jesus. Jesus did not change His enemies, nor did He want the Father to change them. He only wanted forgiveness for those who did wrong.

When one loves as Jesus loved His enemies, he can do good for hate and pray when despised. The process of forgiveness goes on when one takes on the words of Jesus, "Love your enemies." When extending forgiveness to someone that has done harm, love became the passageway for reconciliation. Jesus came into the world because of love. Jesus came through love to seek the lost, regenerate the mind and offer a better way of doing things.[9] To love your enemies is not the norm. It is the exception. Forgiving with the love of Jesus may not be what is expected; yet it is the right thing to do.

As one enters this passageway and passes through the door, he must place a key in the lock of the door and lock it. Then he must throw the key away and not reenter the door of hate and malice. He must enjoy the love created by the Father which flows through the lives of men. This love causes them to love their enemies and binds them to remember that forgiveness is the final form of love.

The whole is equal to the sum of its parts. Love is the whole of one person who sees the wholeness of another person. It starts as part of the sum and spreads itself through the whole to generate the best responses. Love exercises itself continually as part of the cycle of the whole through compassion and feelings. With love it opens the whole person to forgive with the Love of Jesus.[10] Love does not seek to destroy another person. Its purpose is the restoration of the offender with the offended person. There is no desire to shun, embarrass, be self-righteous, play God or exercise control over the offender. God is a loving, caring shepherd of all His flock and each person is a treasure as an expression of His love. Love is an opportunity for discipline of the wrong with long suffering through forgiveness.

The process of forgiveness must be a confrontation with the person that did wrong. Love does not allow one to disregard another. It sets in motion a process for reconciliation. There is no denial of the harm which was done. The harm allows pain and great hurt to surface as a way to recognize that disfellowship has occurred.

When Judas betrayed Jesus for thirty pieces of silver, Jesus was aware of his action and still maintained a relationship with him. When Judas placed the betrayed kiss on Jesus' cheek, He did not push Judas away or show anger. He simply extended His love as a friend to Judas with forgiveness for the terrible acts he had committed. This was not accepted by Judas, and so the silver which he was paid became a greater source of contempt. He had sold a friend over love and forgiveness and the fellowship which Jesus gave with comfort and peace. Never once did Jesus allow His feelings to become selfish and share with the other disciples what Judas was doing. This is a great lesson in love and forgiveness. Too often when one is hurt, a message is sent to others who in turn take up the banner of hate, scorn and revenge. Jesus kept this to Himself and the disciples did not get a chance for disfellowship because of Judas' harmful acts.

Forgiveness with the love of Jesus is a strong bond for which the betrayer could not refuse to recognize. When love with forgiveness is given, it gets rid of excuses, it eliminates past opportunities, it causes one to face the reality that there is something great, true, honest, sincere and worth more than what one can bargain for. When Judas went back to the priests and threw the thirty pieces of silver at their feet. He exclaimed, "I have betrayed innocent blood". He acknowledged his wrong to those from whom he received money. Now, with this act he did not accept or reestablish ties with Jesus, but he went off and hung himself.

It has to be a hard, insane person to dishonor love and forgiveness when it is given for wrong acts perpetrated by him. Judas had the opportunity to carry the act further than he did. "I have betrayed innocent blood", could have been the start of a new fellowship without any rap sheet of past crimes. No reminder of what was done, no cross-examinations by the disciples, just a free pass with love and forgiveness to renew fellowship with the Master.

The love of Jesus allows one person who accepts Jesus as Lord of their life to extend forgiveness without charge or compromise. With Jesus as our example, there is no other option but to love with forgiveness. Jesus went through the process of pain, agony and the loss of friends, who stated they would be with him no matter what the cost. It did not take long for such words to be tested. With the best intention to remain at the side of Jesus, failure was the final frame. With His friends gone and no one to give encouragement for the tasks ahead, Jesus had within Him something strong and vibrant that radiated beyond the concept of the world. Leave me once, never come back. Leave me twice, I'll never take you back. This was not, and is not, the character of Jesus. He set the supreme example of forgiveness with love for man.

How can one not engage others to ease the process of extending forgiveness? Very simply, forgiveness is not a group process; it is an individual process. Jesus did not include the disciples with information on Judas to make forgiveness easier. He accepted full responsibility for His action, at the same time knowing the actions of Judas. Love with forgiveness goes beyond friends and companions. It goes beyond family; it goes directly to one person that causes pain in order to reach the internal existence for life with the intent to destroy all that is within. Then love and forgiveness takes on the burden of recognition of what was, and what is, and still prevails to restoration. One is more important than the agony and grief for life, so important that Jesus in his agony forgave, as one must also do today.

Forgiveness and love are not enough, in principle, for a code of conduct. They must be activated with the greatest strength that one can obtain to give. There must be love and forgiveness. Love holds the person to a rewarding and full relationship. Forgiveness gives freedom to accept a part of the universal love given to man by the Father.

A Christian was overhead saying, "I can't stand alcoholics, bums, nasty dirty people and filthy children in the projects. They have no place with us." The tragedy of this is that she has not seen the real picture of what she was and what she has become. People are shortsighted to their accomplishments and use them as a standard to elevate themselves to be better than others. This will not work with love. Love is not limited to the clean and nice, or to the non-alcoholics, the rich and famous. Love is for all people that need to be accepted. Love brings greater return for the senders when it is given to those who cannot bargain for its affection and have nothing to compensate for its time. It is given because it is due and received, because it is appreciated. Appreciated love is rewarded with a smile and a thank you and can never be forfeited. When love is given for compensation and rewards, it is without merit and has no value. Love and forgiveness are two powerful forces that cannot be side-traced as the proven thing to do. Love must be honest with the accountability that it brings. Love does not react as a negative against a negative. It is always positive against the negative. It supersedes what is expected. It does not look or expect the worse. It may be disappointed with the behavior of the activity, but never allow the activity to create disfellowship. When disfellowship is present there is no love, and sometimes hate may not blossom itself. When one does not show love, there is the attitude of not caring or showing concern. Forgiveness will not provide for this type of attitude. Forgiveness allows for interaction. Love binds the opportunity for interaction and strives for the value of the person to be greater and worth more than all the damages, disappointments, hurts, or losses that can ever be reclaimed. One hurts, another loves, one loves, another receives love and it is planted to grow and develop into another strong force. Forgiveness relieves the account to pay back. If one chooses, so be it. It's even better to indicate that forgiveness is accepted with great mercy.

"For God so loved the world that He gave his only begotten Son, that whosever believeth in Him should not perish, but have everlasting life." God did not love for what He could receive. He loved for what He could give. Love is not given for what it can receive. Love is given for what it can give. A giver of love is one that is in fellowship with God. The giver is grateful for the Son and is pleased to identify with Him because of the forgiveness of sin and the price paid at Calvary. It is sad when one's greatest desire is to be the recipient of love all the time and not give it away. One cannot have a true appreciation of love until it is given away. One cannot feel the full effect of forgiveness until it is given in the place of revenge and malice. If a person is without the love of Jesus with forgiveness, life comes to a standstill. Character becomes flawed, hope becomes dimmed, anger becomes heightened and the desire to renew fellowship is voided.

If one is to go forward there must be a release of the past hurts and losses. To remain is to thrive on those things which do not build character but destroys it. One's character is the whole of himself as seen by others. If it is phony, others will see it for what it is. If it is real, others will accept it for what it is. To be seen will not provide for fellowship. To be accepted through love will generate more love with fellowship.

Forgiveness with love is not designed to separate. Its purpose is to bind an interwoven and rich foundation that withstands the test of time. The love of Jesus has withstood the events of time. It has brought families back together from strife and pain. It has given the weak a change and a chance to become strong. It has created care and concern for the welfare of others about the dollar. Love has changed the self-centered person to one of passion for others. Love has caused a man or woman to die proudly for their country. It has caused a person to fight with every ounce of strength available to him for that which he believes.

Forgiveness with the love of Jesus cleanses a person from sin to become grateful for the mercy that goes along with it. This process is the greatest accomplishment one can achieve. When one accepts the love of Jesus, a foundation to establish that continues to flow. This is an ongoing process within the brotherhood of believers. Jesus so loved people that the sincerity which He offered to them was received as genuine. And as followers of Him, the process must also be sincere.

Love must be so etched in the lives of people that they feel compelled to give it away. It cannot be from the surface of intuition; it must come from the heart of a person. Should one attempt to reason the righteousness of love, it will not work. Love goes beyond reason or duty. It is more powerful when activated with forgiveness.

If one is to continue forgiving, it cannot be based on number. If one is repentive for his actions, forgiveness is due. The hardest question one may ever propose is, "Should I forgive this?" If Jesus had taken the choice of whom, what and where forgiveness with love would be given, what would be man's condition today? A man is paralyzed by a drunk driver. A young mother is raped by an attacker. Are they to love as Jesus loved? Is forgiveness to be given? Sitting on the sideline, one may cheer, "Forgive", but being the victim of the act sets one into motion to wonder if forgiveness is worth it. The only one that can ever answer these questions is the victim. Jesus was a victim by choice. People are victims by the design of others. As a victim of terrible acts, there is no need to be victim with hate and revenge. Forgiveness cannot be resolved as an act. It is a process that may need to occur daily. Forgiveness allows bad people to become good and allows good people the recognition of mercy for the bad behavior from the past. As a victim of bad behavior by another, one does not have to remain a victim of the act with revenge. If revenge sets in, the victim becomes an enraged time bomb ready to explode without guilt or shame to take the life or another person. Too often people are not the recipient of love and forgiveness because it is their choice.

Jesus, with all his love and forgiveness, allows choice. Choice provides the opportunity for personal acceptance or rejection. There is no between the lines. One must choose to forgive the bad that made poor decisions. It is not an easy road, this cannot be denied. But it can be a road to restoration between the offended and the offender. Forgiveness with the love of Jesus works and it is to this end that the frame of reconciliation must be resolved.

In the First Epistle of John 4:14-20, is an affirmation of what love is about as it relates to Jesus. "And we have seen and do testify that the Father sent the Son to be the Saviour of the world. Whosoever shall confess that Jesus is the Son of God, God dwelleth in him, and he in God. And we have known and believed the love that God hath to us. God is love; and he that dwelleth in love dwelleth in God, and God in him. Herein is our love made perfect, that we may have boldness in the day of judgment: because as he is, so are we in this world. There is no fear in love; but perfect love casteth out fear: because fear hath torment. He that feareth is not made perfect in love. We love him, because he first loved us. If a man say, I love God, and hateth his brother, he is a liar: for he that loveth not his brother whom he hath seen, how can he love God whom he hath not seen?"[2] Love cements and restores relationships. As people become more loving, love is recognized as being a part of God. God is love, and as a God of love, there must be the presupposition that Jesus is the Son of God. He then, as the Son of God, is in a relationship with the Father that is captured with love. Love does not present drawbacks. Its greatest desire is the fulfillment of restored relationships between people. Love cannot be denied as a binding force between people and then accepted as one between the Father and Son. Love is of God as with the Son, and a person that extends forgiveness with love is in a unique position to see the growth and maturity it has between offenders and the offended. The first Epistle of John 4:7-8, "Beloved, let us love one another: for love is of God; and every one that loveth is born of God, and knoweth God. He that loveth not knoweth not God; for God is love."[2] If one is to be a part of the process of forgiveness as a receiver or giver, the motivating force must be love. As one gives love it is an expression of what God is all about. In St. John 3:16, "For God so loved the world, that he gave his only begotten Son, that whosoever believeth in him should not perish, but have eternal life."[2] Love is the process of forgiveness in actions for past sins manifested by Jesus for the world. The Son gave his life and through him, there is forgiveness for all that will accept it.

CHAPTER 8

"Father, Forgive Them"

St. Luke 23:34: "Father, forgive them; for they know not what they do."[2] These words spoken by Jesus while on the cross are a petition to the Father for the intercession of His transgressors. Although they had done wrong to Jesus, He prayed and pleaded for their pardon. His plea was not based on the action of evil men, but on His relation with His father to not hold them for their actions. In return, freedom was offered with pardon of sins.[11]

The sins of these men were filled with hate, lies, false accusation, cruelty and blindness. Their objective to destroy blinded them to anything good of the Master with the only focus to get rid of Him to gain self-satisfaction. Why should Jesus intercede for so cruel a group of men? Clearly there is the answer to Jesus to forgive sin through the love He has for man. With forgiveness, each person received the attention to be released from the guilt and pain of wrong to righteous living. These were not choices. Christ was God manifested in the flesh. As such, He had real pain and feeling for those who did wrong.[12]

To be released by Jesus with the forgiveness of sin and then released from personal injury inflicted without cause is an act of forgiveness. Jesus knew that wrong had occurred and He acknowledged and dealt with it. He did not overlook, or wink at sin. He took sin seriously to show forgiveness by the forgiver. There is a need to forgive as Christ forgave. There is no escape for this. One must bear the cost of forgiving and intercede to Christ for the welfare of another soul. Forgiveness is hard, yet the opportunity to forgive cannot be denied.

When one accepts the hurt, pain and loss that accompanies forgiveness, and then intercedes for the welfare of the person who did the wrong, this places one in a great relationship with the Father to know that not only is personal forgiveness extended, but forgiveness is also asked of the Father. Do not charge this to them. Charge it to me.

"Father, forgiven them" is a prayer for men who did physical harm to Jesus. To make such a request for His attackers, Jesus proved that He was about the business of the Father. As such, His great desire was in the service of mankind. This prayer was to remove the consequences of deplorable acts. Spitting on someone is a nasty act, and unwarranted. This was done to Jesus with rough handling by an uncontrolled mob eager to inflict pain. Jesus did not view the mob as a group that needed to get what they had coming. He saw and recognized that they were in need and prayed for their pardon.

When a person or group performs terrible crimes against another person and prayer is given for their benefit without any drawback, this is forgiveness at its best. This allows the offender the chance for restoration for the acts committed and pardon with an opportunity for repentance. The door of opportunity is needed by all that come short of the plan which the Heavenly Father has. Jesus firmly experienced the abuse and provided the correct way to deal with it.

Jesus was not blinded by revenge of His attackers. He recognized them for what they were. They were persecutors and murderers that needed to be forgiven of their sin. Through the words, "Father forgive them", Jesus gave up the right for justice under the law. He gave up the right to reason with them to draw their attention to what they were doing.

And, if He had tried to reason with the mob, what could He have accomplished? His death was their final frame to stop the abuse. The Son of Man was allowed to be treated as a criminal for trying to help the very same people that were against Him.

Sometimes the best of people are kept in darkness of ignorance under the control of others. As such, the actions that they imposed on others are not of their own doing. They are simply carrying out the deeds planted in their minds to do. How sad it is when such deeds enter into the fellowship of men when they perform such feats in the name of God. What gives people courage to kill for good, hate for righteousness, and murder without justification? Perhaps the answer is in selfishness to get what is wanted at any cost. Such people are to be pitied and prayed for on a daily basis.

Oh, what deeper pits we dig when we do not pray for those that make us weep. To get personal strength, there must be prayer for enemies as they hate and persecute without cause. This is a direct focus of what is and what can be done with prayer. Prayer sets in motion a message that there are needs and there is a desire for fulfillment of them.

If there is no tolerance with forgiveness for evil people, what is the need for prayer? Many times when evil deeds are perpetuated against others, there is something within to resist pain and the agony that is being given by the offender. This is normal, because the one thing that people resent is pain. Some pain is necessary for discipline. Even when it may be administered with love, it may not be appreciated.

Rightfully, each of Jesus' attackers, accusers and heads of an illegal court should have received punishment for what they did. But Jesus emptied Himself of such claims. He took a servant's stance. He stood tall without reaching out to fight back. He cared and did not insult His enemies. His love had no condition except to be received. His ministry was a gift of respect, even unto death. The position that He took set Him in high favor with God. Why? Because God values love, God is love. God values caring, because God cares.[13] And the graciousness of Jesus not to have His enemies accounted for their actions, sent a clear message of mercy to have justice dismissed.

Wrong for wrong does not help in the restoration process. The depth of a relationship is really tested when one receives insults and abuses and determines that a loving relationship shall not be broken. Jesus was innocent and did not allow anything to stop the love He had for men no matter what course of action they took. He was innocent of crimes then treated as having committed them. He kept himself from revenge within the boundary of love. Jesus' love did not begin in the sequence of events leading to Calvary. It began with His relationship with the Father. "For God so loved the world that he gave his only begotten Son." Love generates the opportunity to hold on when mistreated. Love issues a plea; I love you too much to allow you this way out. Therefore, I shall go on loving with no misconception about giving it, even at the time when it is not appreciated.

Jesus did not bear a loss; He was hurt by the mob who did not receive His love right away. Yet, He held it above all the wrong and eventually love won. So much so, that an unknown soldier vibrated the words, "Surely He was the Son of God." Love was not alone. As forgiveness entered the picture, there was a great burst of energy and emotion that swept across the world and remains today in the power of forgiveness.

Love with forgiveness gives up personal rights; it yields to maintain a relationship with the person and kindles mercy for evil. The losses which are gone are no longer held and are not included for redemption. If losses are held for redemption, the process of forgiveness is incomplete, because forgiveness releases and moves on to reconciliation, negated of losses.

Forgiveness is a choice to maintaining that which is pulling away or reclaims that which has pulled away. With forgiveness there is pain and a great price for its pondering effects. The process of forgiveness may cause one to have to linger with the consequences of its effect. Yet, for the outcome of disfellowship, forgiveness is not worth being withheld. Is it easy to do? No, it is not! But, the value that it places above the acts of a person is worth more than any man or woman could ever perceive.[14]

Forgiveness with love intercedes between the acts of wrong and the power to get even. It overshadows the wrong and elevates the value of a person to profound recognition above anything that would tend to denounce reconciliation. There is hope within the worst person. Even if vague, there is a desire to be a part of something and be appreciated for personal value. Forgiveness gives freedom with no restrictions to be at ease in a mutual relationship.

In the Savannah Morning News Parade, an article on April 23, 2000 by Andrew Vachss, a writer and attorney who represents abused children, noted: "A particularly pernicious myth for victims of abuse is that healing requires forgiveness of the abusers. This only leads to further victimization." He added, "The abuser has 'no right' to forgiveness; such blessings can only be earned."

The process of forgiveness does not provide for one to earn it. It does not disown the shame and horror of victims. It does not deny the wrong to the innocent and as hard as it is, the abused person shall never have the freedom of life to exist as a person until forgiveness is released to the abusers.

There is a cleansing effect by the abused to offer pardon to one that does not deserve it. It sets in motion for one to be restored even though it is not deserved.

Jesus must be the example from which we base the process of forgiveness. People are hurt so deeply by the wounds of torment, that it is inconceivable for them to even consider forgiveness of the offender. When a hole is dug so deep that as one looks up there is only the abuser above him. With no hope but to hate and get even, there is no satisfaction for life except that the abuser receives greater pain than those afflicted. Ellen Halbert, a holocaust survivor and the Nobel Laureate, said in prayer at the 50th anniversary of the liberation of Auschwitz, "God of forgiveness, do not forgive those murders of Jewish children here." Forgiveness is not an issue for debate, nor is it an act to be denied because of the horror of the situation. The words spoken by Ellen Halbert rip into the internal being of those who experienced such madness. Those millions of people who suffered and the ones that performed these terrible deeds are dead. There is no process to be completed between parties. The process for forgiveness must be for the living to give and receive, and the burden must be assisted with the help of Jesus in prayer to commence any hope for a change to occur.

Jesus prayed to the Father to forgive His enemies. Somehow the realization for the survival of one who experienced unimaginable sequence after sequence of terrible acts to even relate to forgiveness may seem without merit. But, for the survival of all the wrong committed against Him, forgiveness was given away.

Jesus did not give a choice; He set the condition for the offender that committed wrong acts. The merit of forgiveness is far greater than the torch of getting even. As this torch burns, it eliminates each day of peace with the Master that can never be regained. Jesus forgave in prayer to the Father. People in all avenues of life that hurt to the heart must also forgive. Heart pain is a great thrust that is not easily set aside with forgiveness. There may be pain that is tearful and grief not spoken, yet the heart must function with the limit of Jesus' words, "Father forgive them." To forgive will release the heart from being in pain, to receiving joy and happiness. (More about joy will be given in Chapter 10.) There is no greater pain that hurts to the core of the heart when one is expected to rise above and set the person free who caused the hurt. What a call! What a job! What a process! By failing to give forgiveness, one will not be able to have the approval of the Father with the Son to receive forgiveness.

As in the process of respiration, cells take in oxygen and give off the product carbon dioxide which is not needed and is expelled. As this process continues, the growth of the cells develops and more cells are developed. If a person takes in the love of Jesus and His forgiveness, then the product of hate, revenge and all other hurts that are not needed by the body will be expelled and the body will continue to grow spiritually, physically and mentally.

With all the strength one may have to generate the process of forgiveness, there needs to remain one fact. It is not within the strength of a person to forgive. It is with the assistance of Jesus to forgive. The forgiveness of sin is not within the capacity of man. This is reserved for God. Forgiveness is not an act of man; it is a divine process by the Heavenly Father. This in itself establishes a need for prayer for the offender and the offended, to seek assistance to begin the process. Sometimes the offended confuses crime with sin and seeks to hold one in contempt for sins committed. There is no capacity for such. Crimes are punished by laws of the land. Sins are punished by the Father. Through the process of forgiveness the innocent victim must look beyond personal gratitude to seek to be in the will of God. What will God have me do, remains a question to be answered daily.

When sin is committed that is against the laws of God, he alone can offer freedom from this sin to move forward with life. Forgiveness does not end with sin; it extends to the offended who in turn reciprocates it to the offenders for all the harm done in the past and awaits its opportunity for the future.

Righteous living is what Christ wanted in the lives of men. Forgiveness provides the person who accepts this process the opportunity to reach the fullest endeavor possible by being reconciled with Christ. If one is to be restored with Christ, there must be the daily plea, "Father, forgive me as I forgive them." To give forgiveness there must be an experience of having been forgiven by Jesus Christ. Love keeps the process in motion. So must it be. There is no alternative. When it is done, victory awaits those that are involved in the process of forgiving.

People's lives are affected for long periods of time because of three words: "Father forgive them," or more personally, "Father forgive me." For a person to make such a request there must be the expressed desire to give up a burden or habit that has plagued them with no results. To acknowledge the need for forgiveness, hold one accountable from that point forward. There cannot just be an act to please. This begins a process in recognition that a part of life is overwhelmed with loose ends that need mending.

There may be times when there is a visible effect of the need to get assistance from the Father. Other times, a person may be so involved with the problem that he cannot separate the act from the individual that did the harm. A person may begin a process of reconciliation before these words are spoken. The mind can process information so rapidly that it is hard to keep up. With this incredible feature, information can be hindered, ended or stops the process of forgiveness. Head knowledge is not the answer. Heart knowledge is the cure.

During the time that Jesus was on Earth, He established close relationships with His disciples. After seeing how Jesus healed and changed the lives of people, one would easily perceive that they would follow and remain loyal to Him. Peter made this promise with good intention that he would never leave the side of Jesus. A little while later he even attacked another with a sword in defense. But this same Peter disassociated himself when Jesus needed him. Such is the way of people when there is a need for someone to stand up. Yet Jesus, with His forgiving spirit, did not hold Peter and abandon him for the wolves. Jesus, in the place of hurt and physical pain did not place in jeopardy the lives of any of His followers. He accepted his fate and went on with the plan given to Him by God. As Jesus worked with His disciples, He knew them and knew the personality of Peter, more so than Peter knew himself. Yet within this love that he had, there was something about Peter that needed to be kept intact. This was reconciliation.

Jesus is about reconciliation as He extends forgiveness to man. When a break of unity occurs, there is the need for mending a rightful restoration even when there is rebellion. Jesus broke down the middle wall of partition and gave man a direct line for restoration. As long as there is division, there is a need for peace through Jesus for the consequence of wrong actions. When Christ died on the cross, He brought peace that went from Him to every man that accepts His plan of forgiveness.

It must also be noted that the death of Christ was not in vain. It was for sinners with love and forgiveness. Yet when Jesus died on the cross, He had reconciliation for man. What power He has! He conquered death as a way of acknowledging to the God of Heaven and earth that He is supreme. As the supreme, there is a right to have certain power and control in the fulfillment of getting men to be reconciled to Jesus.

Even with this process, there is no demand that it shall be. There is always the invitation to be reconciled rather than the demand. When two people are reconciled through the process of forgiveness and love, this must not be an attribute claimed by man. Credit must always be given to its rightful owner as a process of God in a direct relationship with His Son, Jesus. When it is not used correctly, as an extension of the love of God, forgiveness becomes just a word with no ground for support.

When Jesus said these words, "Father forgive them", the sting of justice was removed for all those that were in conflict with Him. This became a prayer of intercession for sin which He wanted for the whole world. This prayer was not given exclusively for the men that day that did wrong. It sounded a redemptive voice across time not yet experienced by man. Yet man, then and now, would be in need of the forgiveness of Jesus. It remains to be an important factor that Jesus experienced excruciating pain and agony on the cross, and through love asked for forgiveness. This would remind a person today that from the worst experiences that we go through, forgiveness is possible. Jesus felt from the human side betrayal, disassociation and disfellowship of his friends. He knew real pain and the lingering effects that it could bring. Therefore, He does not allow for disfellowship. He wants fellowship without restrictions. Yet He must be free of the torch of resentment and ridicule. In the place of justice, mercy is extended. It would seem fair that justice should have been given to those men that allowed themselves to be used by those trying to protect their economic interest.

One's economic status and values for wealth must become secondary if forgiveness is to be the avenue for reconciliation. Jesus did not allow the soldier at the foot of the cross gambling for His clothes, or the men of the Sanhedrin that hardened themselves to righteousness, or Herod that scorned Him as a magician, to prevent the process of forgiveness from being in existence. All failed because as Jesus went to the cross, He in His agony was responsive to the call and plea of one who said, "Remember me."

What words were used to get the attention of Jesus? The thief did not ask for forgiveness and in effect he received justice for his action while Jesus received injustice for His action. Forgiveness was so powerful that it was given because one spoke from the heart. The thief, by his humble nature and acknowledgement of who Jesus was, also received a victorious celebration with the father in Heaven. Forgiveness is a release from the old to the new. The man was nailed to the cross as a thief and removed through forgiveness as a child of the King, with the words, "This day thou shall be with me in paradise."

One's actions can override any words that could be spoken. It has been stated that, "actions speak louder than words" and so the words of a thief rendered him guilty. But the action of forgiveness through Jesus rendered him free. The thief became free from crime, insults, physical pain and torment. Humiliation was supposed to place its verdict of guilty for sins committed. Forgiveness interceded with love and said, "No more. You are free to be better than you were before. You are free to be released of all obligations through mercy and love." One thief, because he did not seek for selfish gain, received life while the other thief sought to gain freedom.

Selfish desires and attitude prevents the process of forgiveness from going forth as it should. The words of the thief on the cross will remain in the history of time, "This Man has done nothing wrong." And through it all He remains and should be called that which He is, "Jesus".

In Luke, Chapter 15, verses 11-32, the parable of the lost son is recorded. It is with keen interest that throughout the story the actions of the father as he deals with both sons are important. One son asked for and received his inheritance, then threw it away. The older son remained at home and continued to work for the father. After the younger son left home, the father sat and waited for his return with love and forgiveness. Upon squandering everything he had, the son came to himself, and did not blame or condemn anyone for his actions. He stated, "I will go and ask to be a hired servant." The father, because of love and compassion, did not allow such a thing. The lost need visible recognition of fellowship back into the family. There can be no second-guessing; it is real. It is worth it all to be restored with honor. Standing on the sideline, the other brother refused to be a part of the fellowship and reconciliation. Even though that was his choice, the process of restoration must prevail. A son lost is not restored. Another son also lost, did not even know it, nor did he seek fellowship with a father who loves all.[15]

Jesus, as the Father in the Prodigal Son, did not stop one from choice. With choice came consequences. There was no mention by the father that, "I knew this would happen. Look at you now." The opportunity of repentance was accepted on its merit. Forgiveness was given and the son now lost was saved. Another son who thought he was saved was lost. Grace was available for the two by the father; one chose fellowship, the other denied its value and worth. When the son returned home, he was renewed and restored. One must never forget that the process of forgiveness does not end with an act of happiness when one returns to the family of God. Forgiveness must be the process by which the offender and the offended must be reconciled.

Forgiveness cannot be substituted by someone for another. The process forbids one to speak for another person. Each as an independent agent must give and receive it. It is too valuable and worthy to be tossed around by one for another. It requires one to take time if needed rather than act in hast with no real superficial pain. The pain must be so deep that the mind says no while the heart opens itself for a historical awakening. Forgiveness is the essence upon which love thrives and grows deeper and richer. The giver of forgiveness accepts it as a way of getting from anything that binds and keeps life from walking down the avenues of reward and contentment. The offender sees and accepts forgiveness as the opportunity that gives justice a back seat and mercy a seat of honor.

One may argue that forgiveness cannot be with honor. There is no other way for it to seep into the lives of people. There was no one that could take the place on the cross and offer forgiveness except Jesus. The process is too pure for any man to start its reconciliation. It is too holy to be accountable to man. It is too powerful to be maintained by man. It is too needful to be kept in the mind of men that starve for it so badly.

To say the word, "Father" is recognition to whom prayer should be addressed. It defines a responsibility of who is able to deal with the pain that is needed for the process of completion. It also indicates that one is unable to bring peace or solution to the pain generated by another person. "Father" is a plea for help. It makes known that one is before him to obtain grace and mercy. It is not a plea with anger and malice. It is one with compassion. "Father" is a world with sincerity and reverence before one that is above all other. It is a call with the full attention of the mind, soul and body. It is a plea so serious that if the attention is not solicited, there is no other way by which the problem may be resolved. There is no desire to seek any other method or personality, because one knows it would be hopeless. The process of forgiveness begins with the Father. He understands it is the need and the reason for one to seek it rather than seek revenge. He is glad for appeal. His ears are sensitive to the caller. There is nothing that is found between Heaven and Earth that can interfere with the reception of these vibrations. He is never too busy to bother, rather He is constantly responding, "I hear the call my child. State your case."

The words "forgive them", "forgive him" or sometimes "forgive me", specifies the reason for a plea. The plea is not for justice; it is for pardon. The pleas make no summary for losses or pain. It is from one who knows the offender and sets in motion the opportunity for him to walk away a free man. There cannot be a retrial; no new appeal will be necessary. There is no need for a paid attorney, because in this plea, he is unwarranted. He cannot fill the request that is in the heart of the offended to prescribe for the offender. The plea relieved the offender of the need to fight back. These words are of such magnitude that they may be repeated again. These words specify the need to one that has heavenly resources available to relate to the plea. The plea is not selfish; it is straightforward. No playing around. It states the problem in simple terms. There is no urging by a crowd. The plea is between "Father" and one who has become a child of the Father with forgiveness and love. One then knows the awesome ability of its power. One has experienced the glow of peace that the word brings. When spoken, the words are for a binding, restored relationship that is alive with love and reconciliation. These words are needed, for the time, to get above hurt and pain. These words see the person above the character of what he was to what he can become. The acts committed are not a part of the agenda and does not play any role in the request to the Father. This request is open. Only the person making the plea may use it again. There are no restrictions on how many times it may be used. A disciple of Jesus tried to put the process completed at seven. Jesus stated, "No! Not seven, but 70 x 7." It is to be given as many times as a repentive person is in need of it. This plea does not stop when not requested by offenders. It must be used as a daily plea for restoration with the Heavenly Father.

The strength of words has been so strong that a dying man in his final hour was rescued from a painful cross with the words, "Verily I say unto thee, today shall thou be with me in paradise." This was lifted to another life without the word "forgive" being used. But, the attitude through the humbleness of the heart made it worthwhile for forgiveness to be given to free a dying man.

In the parable of the prodigal son there is a departure from the father. As people are involved in sin, there is a departure from God. In the departure from God many things become apparent. There is a distance from God of which there is no fellowship. There is a need of want that cannot be filled. There is the need to substitute life for the real thing for that which is hopeless. There is madness and there is a great need to be readmitted into the family of the Father. Forgiveness opens the door for one to be filled with love and assurance that the Heavenly Father cares. The greatest thing that a person can have is the opportunity of fellowship and restoration with the Father without restriction. Such was the case with the son when he returned home. There was rejoicing for the son that had returned home. By his action the son demonstrated that he was sorry for what he had done. And the acceptance by the father to put shoes on his feet, a robe on his body and a ring on his finger said in effect, you are home.

When one is forgiven by the Father, there is a change in life. A merry way instead of a sinful one helps the forgiven to know that he is appreciated. The sad part of this story is that the son who was in the house with the father all the time did not appreciate the father welcoming his brother home. It is a sad thing when forgiveness has been given and someone comes and tries to undermine what has taken place. The older son did not want anything to do with his baby brother. Jesus reminded us that a person that is well does not need a physician; only those that are hurting without food and clothes and have not accepted Jesus. These are the ones for whom He died and these are the ones for whom forgiveness is needed. Forgiveness provides an avenue for the departed to return home in fellowship with all the blessings of home that are available to everyone.

Forgiveness gets down to the worst and offers light. It does not seek to remind or penalize. It is the process by which a person may fellowship with another through mercy and love. It is the process by which all men may be forgiven of their sins and have fellowship with Jesus Christ.

CHAPTER 9

The Holy Spirit and Forgiveness

The Holy Spirit is not a mere influence from God. He is God Himself in the spiritual operation and manifestation of truth. The Holy Spirit comes to be in the hearts of believers to communicate the work of the Father. It therefore becomes necessary for one to submit to the will of the Holy Spirit. Submission is necessary to the will of God as one receives guidance to ascribe to forgiveness.[16]

Forgiveness must cause one to believe in the power of the Holy Spirit as a direct link with the Father and Son, and then be guided in the process to extend forgiveness without compromise. If the Holy Spirit is going to help, one must obey the word of God and know that the Holy Spirit only conveys that which is already in Scripture. The word is given in Luke 17:3-4 which is spoken by Jesus. "Take heed to yourselves: If thy brother trespass against thee, rebuke him; and if he repent, forgive him. And if he trespass against thee seven in a day, and seven times in a day turn again to thee, saying, I repent: thou shalt forgive him."[2]

The Scripture is in direct relation to the Holy Spirit which executes the Divine purpose of the Father. As Jesus speaks, He is not in disfellowship with the Holy Spirit. The Holy Spirit, the Father and the Son speak equally that forgiveness is to be available not one time, but as many times as one seeks forgiveness with a repentant heart. One who remains under the unction of the Holy Spirit is certain to act in a way that is truthful and honest. In man's weakness to forgive, the Holy Spirit becomes an accommodation to that weakness.

The Holy Spirit takes one through the processes essential in forgiveness. The Holy Spirit leads in difficult times with tenderness, humbleness, faithfulness, truth and holiness. He leads away from error into truth and provides a perfect relationship of peace by forgiving, even when it is not merited. The Holy Spirit is right, He is truth and He is a guide that stands alone without error and complete. For the offended it leads beyond the circumstances and events to a holy and meaningful relationship with the Father. The Holy Spirit is the supreme advocate in the lives of men to direct them in doing what is right. Forgiveness is right.

When one is in fellowship with Jesus and remains in submission, the Holy Spirit will work. Then there is an opportunity to be humbled by the grace given by Jesus. Through His grace under the Holy Spirit, one becomes strengthened with confidence as proclaimed through the Word. Thus, forgiveness is not for the proud. It is an acceptance that with the Holy Spirit forgiveness is a continual process that is repeated many times. Even seventy times seven.

The Holy Spirit is God in action. He does not exist independently of God. He is personal and a permanent manifestation of God. Christ spoke through the Spirit as He worked with His disciples, and many times they did not comprehend what was being said. Even the Jews read the scripture in their synagogue and they did not understand all that was read to them. It was as if a veil covered the truth for which the disciples did not understand. Yet, as Jesus spoke through the Spirit and the Spirit made Himself know to them, there was understanding.

The Holy Spirit is of God and Christ. There cannot be a separation because they are one. There is not a Spirit of God and of Christ. One Spirit is enough for the unity of God and Christ. It is most important to understand that the process of forgiveness was the Spirit of God in Jesus which gave Him power to love His enemies and show forgiveness in the most grueling situations. Christ operated in the human flesh and the Father sent the Holy Spirit to comfort Him in the time of trial and loneliness. This same resource and power is available to all in fellowship with Jesus. These powers recognize forgiveness to be the identification for the process of reconciliation.

As there is a unity of God, Spirit and the Son, so must there be a unity of fellowship through the process of forgiveness. It is without merit to say it cannot be. "Christ and the Spirit are really God in His self-determined mode of operation in the creation, redemption and sanctification of the world. In every activity of each of the three 'person' of the Trinity, it is always the one and the same God who acts. That is to say, the personae must not be rigidly separated from one another and identified with particular divine functions (i.e. creating, redeeming, sanctifying), for the entire personae act in every divine work. It is clear then to regard the work of the ascended Christ and the work of the Holy Spirit as inseparably and individually the activity of the one God, whose age long plan for man's redemption and restoration is now made known, as in a mystery, to the enlightened eyes of those who believe in Christ."[17]

The process of forgiveness has always been available for man to use. Its purpose is to redeem broken relationships and set in motion pure motives of operation with the assistance of the Holy Spirit. As the Holy Spirit works in the lives of man to forgive and accept the process of forgiveness, the Father and Son are also at work. This is important to know throughout this chapter. As the term Holy Spirit is used, it is not the intent to separate Him as a source void of the Christ and the Father.

Forgiveness is a precious divine source that hinges on a person's relationship with Christ. He cannot be induced at will by one who has been betrayed by the actions of another. This is a heavenly resource and must be respected as such. Forgiveness will not be a part of the foul degenerate mind that attempted to use Him for personal gain. There is no pleasure in this kind of action. There is no love here and no reconciliation to be gained. The Holy Spirit as a Divine Personality cannot be a part of that which is evil. He will only be a part of that which is honest and right.

When Joseph was sold by his brothers, he missed out on family gatherings. The active love of his father was void of his presence. And when the opportunity was given to him to get even, Joseph chose the right way of forgiveness. It was not the easy way, nor was it without pain. But it was the right thing to do for the time and place. Forget what was lost or denied. The Holy Spirit was at work to give mercy instead of justice. And later at the death of Joseph's father, there was a recurrence in the minds of the brothers. Surely, Joseph would remember what they did and he would get them. What the brothers did not know was that Joseph never forgot their terrible deed; he simply did not allow it to interfere with a love restoration relationship that superseded personal feelings. Forgiveness does not vent anger or hatred on what is, what could and how could you have. It deals with the time at hand. The present is so valuable that it will not tolerate anything or anyone from being within the bounds of reconciliation. When the brothers approached Joseph with their thoughts, he was hurt by the fact that they thought he would get back at them. It is one thing to be hurt for pains of wrong deeds, but there is a greater hurt when pains are perceived to come from that which is good. The forgiveness by Joseph was not only for his brothers; it was for their families. No one was to suffer for the actions of others. No one was to live in fear. No one was to even experience any pain, because the Spirit was at work in the life of Joseph. Through these acts of forgiveness, Joseph did not become less of a man. He did not have to take a back seat in his position. Nor was he trying to prove how good he could be for the past wrong deed done to him by his brothers.

Forgiveness did not begin with Joseph's brothers. It started at the house of his Master, Potiphar whose wife falsely accused him. In addition, the chief butler forgot to return a favor. Joseph was already involved in the process of forgiveness. Upon becoming second in command, Potiphar's wife was at his mercy. Likewise so were the men in jail with him and the butler. All were at the call of Joseph to remind them of their wrong deeds. There was never a time when Joseph sought them out to make known, "I am he whom you mistreated and caused great pains." Joseph was not overcome by pain. He overcame them with acts of kindness, love and humility. If one is to travel through the process of forgiveness, he shall not be burdened with the guilty load of pain caused by another person.

If one is to be used by the Holy Spirit to activate forgiveness, there must be a cleansing of the body from evil, and a cleansing of the mind from revenge. There cannot be darkness with light. Forgiveness is light and revenge is darkness. The two cannot be together for reconciliation. There must be one or the other. Joseph became and wanted to be partners with his brothers. This was made possible through restoration. Enjoy what I enjoy, eat what I eat; the land I use is the land you shall use. Nothing shall be lacking on my part to be in fellowship with you. You are now restored! The brothers of Joseph were called what they were, his brothers. They were not subordinates because of the position he held which was higher than theirs. He used the position, with love, for reconciliation to bring about harmony in a family ruined by lies and jealousy. This jealousy had to be stopped. The love of one brother with forgiveness under the guide of the Holy Spirit made that which was intended to be bad become good; even for the offenders. Should Joseph's brothers enjoy the benefit of luxury that he could provide? Should they be protected by the power given to him, though he was not protected? The question is not "should", but the answer is, he did, because the Holy Spirit will anoint that which is good to do good.

Because of the partnership established by Joseph with his brothers, communication became the basis for ongoing relationships. Communication brought the brothers together as colleagues for the good of the family. Their communication with each other, which was encouraged by Joseph, became in effect a communication with the Holy Spirit through the process of forgiveness. In a partnership there are common goals for the welfare of all concerned. The common goal is fellowship with excellent communi-cation. It cannot stop. With communication from the heart there is a comfort zone that stops suffering and discomfort. When this occurs there is the resource of power that continues to flow on a need basis.

In the process of forgiveness through partnership with the offended and the offender, there is a mutual agreement that this process will work. If given by the offended and not accepted by the offender, this does not make the process less valid, nor does it degrade and take anything away from the one who is hurt from the experience. Forgiveness with love is to be given away. It is not at the expense of one to decide if it will be received or not. It is given under the guide of the Holy Spirit with grace and mercy. For the offended, he has fellowship with Jesus. With the offender, there is an opportunity for fellowship with a brother, in love approved by the Spirit.

There are blessings for all that share in the process of forgiveness. It is for the humble and is without monopoly by anyone. The Holy Spirit serves as the helper and witness. He also is the teacher, guide and strength of all that become submissive to His will. It is His greatest desire that there be fellowship after the experience of pain. He rejoices in two beings reconciling above things and positions. He knows that forgiveness works because He has seen its effect since the beginning of time. He is keenly aware that the process will be invalid with personal interest, lingering grief, worldly ambition, deceit, lies, pride, position, the desire to be in control and the opportunity to get even.

Through the Holy Spirit, the weak become strong. The ordinary man, with forgiveness, becomes strong as a receiver and as a giver. There are no restraints on what one may become. Restoration and reconciliation are the key players. As the process of forgiveness continues and growth occurs for one or more, jealously does not become a problem. It becomes a daily task and an opportunity for one to look within himself and realize that the credit is not his to gain. It is from a heavenly power that is far superior to all men combined in power and strength. The process as an act of the heavenly host must be kept within that frame. If one attempts or seeks to go outside this perimeter, the consequences can be terrible for all parties involved.

When one considers why there is so much hate, bitterness and contempt for pain that is unwarranted, there is a need for the cycle to be broken. It cannot be so without assistance of the Holy Spirit. This power is not limited to anyone except the person that allows it to be. Physical torment to one's family and friends can become worse than if the pain was inflicted personally. There is a sense of pride for one to achieve when it can be said, "I'll get the person who did this to you, and you will never have to worry again. I'll take care of you." The tragedy of all this is that sometimes the one offering the protection for the victim becomes worse off than the victim. Instead of things and circumstances getting better, all involved become entangled in a web of pity, anger, revenge and the will to get even.

Men that are in a revenge mode do not become open to the Holy Spirit. They are in a war with themselves, the person they are trying to destroy and anyone else that stands in their way. Personal resources will be used up to get even. Lost time with children and a spouse becomes obsolete. Their only will for life is to get even. When men get in this condition, they are in a very dangerous situation. They could get revenge at a much greater cost than they could ever imagine.

A man became crippled after being struck by a hit-and run- driver. He spent money and time looking for the driver to get even. He left his children and wife to follow every lead he could to catch his enemy. Going from state to state and city to city, all trails eventually lead to a dead end. One night while at a hotel, he received word that the man he was looking for was at the same place as him. At last he would get his revenge. His years of tracking would be over. In the meantime, he had received word that he could be cured of the crippling malformation that had him in so much physical pain. Not a chance would be given for freedom of physical pain when there was a greater pain in his heart. That night he shot the man that had crippled him years earlier. Sweet release, freedom and joy were all his to claim, only to find out that the man he had shot was the one who had developed a cure for his handicap. As the doctor lay dying, he told of a man he had hit in an accident and tried to find. He had placed on record that he had committed this act and would not hold a man in contempt for what he did to him. With his last word he simply said, "He has suffered enough. Let him be free." He offered him pardon for taking his life. What is it that drives a person to hate when the power of forgiveness can resolve the problem? Nothing is more misguided than a man blinded by hate and revenge with normal eyesight. And yet, he cannot see the light of life for seeing the darkness of revenge.

The Holy Spirit sets men apart from revenge by choice. He who does not choose to be free will not be free. Revenge does not allow the Holy Spirit to work. It prevents mutual consent and does not allow two to become one in reconciliation with love. There is dishonor and lack of power that one may feel inclined to have as the dagger of hate is plunged into the back of another. Revenge does not fight fair; it attacks from any side. It seeks to have an advantage any way that it can get it. Its only goal is to satisfy self. This is impossible because if man had it within his power to provide self-satisfaction, there would be no need for the Holy Spirit. He would reach within his power at his whim and restore happiness, joy and peace. But, with all that he has available to him, he cannot and does not have the power to provide for himself. Nor does he have the option to reel in fellowship of another and release it at his command. This power is limited within the restrain of heavenly power. Man can get a great awakening of how pleasurable forgiveness is through the power of the Holy Spirit. He can come to a place in life where he thinks more of people than of things, he thinks more of a man's fellowship without restrictions, he sees no standard except that which is already in motion through love. He sees no author of forgiveness except through the mercy of the Son, approved by the Father with the Holy Spirit. Time becomes but an instant opportunity to do that which is right, orderly and holy under the power of the Holy Spirit.

When a person seeks to render forgiveness for pain he becomes subjected to the power of the Holy Spirit. With power comes authority and effectiveness to accept a person as a brother in a sphere of love and respect. The power that is obtained is not given to man to gain greater control to be in charge of people. This power is given for man to be in control of himself. When one is in control, there is a greater chance to respond in the right way when evil deeds are activated toward him. This power stops man from being the problem or becoming a part of the problem. Through the power of forgiveness, there is a great need to face issues and seek to bring them to the forefront for the purpose of reconciliation. It's fair to recognize that this power cannot be stopped at the surface of one's mind. It must penetrate to the heart for the purpose of binding two in love.

Throughout time, men and women have lied, cheated and used all kinds of personal resources to gain power. Wars have been fought for the purpose of control. Even countries have been at war with one another. The basic issue is power to control or power to enforce. A person may submit to another because of the great force of power that is placed on him. Or, he may rebel and fight to resist the dominant conquering force. Lives are wasted because of the desire to have or gain power. Even worse is the power that has been obtained and is used to exploit and cause greater problems in the name of righteousness. Then there is the harm that has resulted within the fellowship of the body of believers, because of misguided or abused power.

The power of forgiveness under the will of the Holy Spirit does not seek to dethrone the will of a person. He does not glorify in one being defeated by the conquering foe. His goal and purpose is the acknowledgement of having experienced unwarranted or warranted pain and give to the offender the mercy and right of being pardoned. This is power at its best. This is the foundation upon which families, churches, nations and individuals can function. Nothing is better than when two unlike forces can overcome the law of physics and come together rather than be repelled by their negative forces and attitudes that hinder fellowship.

With the Holy Spirit there is peace and honor with contentment through fellowship. Respect is given even when one does not accept or want the process of forgiveness that is binding through fellowship. Fellowship is so important in forgiveness that it does not give options for the will of being successful. It does not cater to the call of power. It does not accept the fact that a person is hopeless and does not have the desire to begin the process of forgiveness. This course of fellowship tries to get one to be aware of the downfall of the present situation, accept the facts for what they are and seek to move away from the pits of being and doing nothing. The Holy Spirit does not work with cipher. He works with people. People are His resources and the power that He has is transmitted within the hearts of people to make their lives vigorous and filled with love. The love that they enjoy becomes a foundation of greatness in its true form. No person is any greater than the control he has over himself to help someone that has caused him harm. When the words were spoken, "Love your enemies, do good to them which hate you,"[2] Jesus was stating heavenly principles which will keep and transform the lives of man.

In Luke 6:27-28, the words continue with, "Bless them that curse you, and pray for them which despitefully use you."[2] These are the expected behavior mandated by Jesus Christ in fellowship with the Father and the Spirit. It must be. There is no choice. Verses 35-37 place a summation on the power of fellowship that is needed for restoration: "But love ye your enemies, and do good, and lend, hoping for nothing again; and your rewards shall be great, and ye shall be the children of the Highest: for he is kind unto the unthankful and to the evil. Be ye therefore merciful, as your Father also is merciful. Judge not, and ye shall not be judged: condemn not, and ye shall not be condemned: forgive, and ye shall be forgiven."[2]

These verses outline the teachings of Jesus to call attention to the need to be honest and fair. There must be forgiveness to those that have been harmful. Personal rights must become secondary and the law must not be used as a source to become an advantage for the offended person. Love must be exercised and given to the person that does harm. With good deed, prayer must be offered, and the excitement of wishing the offender well must be a priority. To give love to be loved is of no value, but to love one whom you hate is a chance to intercede with God on one's behalf. There is no repayment for doing good. Something better is available, and that is great a reward from the heavenly Father. Mercy is to be given to be received and forgiveness is to be given for one to become a recipient of it. To forgive men of their wrong deeds is to have the love of God. The principle to be applied in all of this is that kindness is to be given for hate; love is to be given when one is despised. There may not be any pay for doing good, yet the Spirit of God is keenly aware of this. The only loser is the person that does not fall under this guidance to become the best that Christ wants him to become.

A person may be brilliant, well learned and versed in scripture and not be in a mode of forgiveness that is mandated by God. This being the case, there cannot be any illumination in the lives of such a person until there is a need and willingness to come under the authority of the Holy Spirit. It is the Holy Spirit that will bring spiritual things to man to make him more accountable to God, himself and his brothers. Forgiveness falls within the spiritual realm that warrants men to have a relationship with God and a relationship with other men. This is essential because if forgiveness is to be a vital part of the person's growth and maturity, there must be recognition of whom and where the authority lies for the completion of the process.

At this point it is essential to understand that the Holy Spirit does not work in the lives of sinners. The God of Heaven and Earth did not have Jesus die on the cross for foolishness. There was pain, toil, sweat, hurt and suffering for the salvation of men. It is therefore worthy to note that the Holy Spirit is essential in the Christian family. He is a source of help for them to do greater work. What one once believed, did and received by way of knowledge and gifts does not inspire the Holy Spirit to move. When Christ left the disciples to reclaim His heavenly home, He told them that because of His departure from Earth, they would receive a comforter which would be the Holy Spirit. These men were to be affected in a dynamic way because the Holy Spirit was to abide forever. He was to dwell in them as disciples of Jesus because of their controlled lives. He was not for the world to toy and play with. He came to reprove the world of sin, righteousness and judgment. Then there is special anointing for those that are under His influence. He takes special interest in their needs, therefore He will teach in all things and guide into all truths. He shall testify of Jesus, He shall glorify Jesus, He shall show you all things and He shall receive of the things of Jesus. "Ye shall receive power, after that the Holy Ghost is come upon you."

Jesus is very specific on the purpose of the Holy Spirit. He did not pull any punches. There was harmony between the Son and the Father. Final approval had been made. The only thing left was the activation as told by Jesus. On the day of Pentecost, He came forth upon men and women and they were not the same. The outlook on life was to represent He that was dwelling in them. Fear was out-classed. Closed tongues for righteousness to speak became loose. Boldness in the work of the Master was primary. He dwells in each person and He is a guide for truth and glory endowed with power.

The Holy Spirit in the process of forgiveness works through people that are in the will of God. Their life takes on special meaning. There is the need to represent Him that guides and teaches the power of truth with love. The same love is needed when disfellowship occurs. In extended forgiveness, one is in fellowship with Jesus. The lifestyle is to do all things through Him, by Him, with Him and of Him. A person of this magnitude is not a fly-by-night trying to make a name for himself. He is working and doing that which has been approved in heaven, demonstrated by the Son and made available to any who are forgiven of their sins.

The Holy Spirit is a divine Person; He is of heaven. There is no place that can bar His presence. Sin in the lives of men will not allow Him to dwell within the soul of man.

There cannot be any misconception about this. He stands above sin. He has the capacity to be everywhere. He knows everything. He cannot be outrun. There is no machine that has as much power as He has. Books are nothing new to Him. He is the author of knowledge and wisdom. He has a personality that only a Christian saved by grace and mercy can appreciate.

He works with the person that offers forgiveness to give power and strength for all injuries. He does not leave one to trouble himself on where He is or His availability. His presence is felt. The knowledge that is needed is known. The power to overcome is granted. The love that is needed to be given to the offender is not vague. It is open because the Holy Spirit does not dwell inside a person to make him less accountable. He makes one more accountable to God with thanksgiving and praise. The opportunity for forgiveness is cherished in the life of the offended. He knows the work and trust of the Master. He does not see forgiveness as a burden. He may not understand all that there is to know in its process, but the Holy Spirit with love, compassion and truth fixes the heart to say "trust me" when you cannot see. "Follow me as your guide. Let my teaching come into your heart and the forgiveness that you give will be eternal with rewards from Heaven."

Forgiveness with the Holy Spirit is a heavenly process. It is not a sham or a one event act. It goes on, and each time it is needed, it extends with love. Forgiveness does not ride on the waves of how many times it reaches out to the same person repeatedly. As many times as one repents, the doors of mercy are open to say, come in. It is aware that its existence in the life of a person is not based on goodness. It is based on the mercy that was ordained in heaven for all who would come boldly to the throne of grace.

Forgiveness with the Holy Spirit is pure. There is nothing that can hinder it except sin. It is too high above the mind of man to be controlled by him. Man needs His power of strength. He does not need man. When man is under His authority, he is humbled because he is inadequate without such power. When man is in a weakened state, as imperfect as he is, He intercedes to the Father on his behalf. Man in his emotion and burst of anger may not want to do as he should. Then the Holy Spirit reminds him of his duty and responsibility. There is no shoving to force the action of man, only a gentle touch to say, this is not the way. Change your plan, for I am the guide for your life. Listen to my voice and you will continue to experience fellowship. With the Holy Spirit, there is fellowship and as He dwells in the heart of the believer, there is continuous fellowship that the disbelievers do not understand.

He is not swayed by emotion. He is touched when one is repentant and seeks to do all that is possible to remain in the will of the Father.

The believer of forgiveness is touched and empowered through the Holy Spirit. He does not sway, although the judgment of the world says it is the correct thing to do. The world as dominated by Satan is of his control. There is no bond between him and the Holy Spirit. His role is one of self-gain, get what you can at the expense of others. Satan hates forgiveness. He does not want fellowship. The greater the problem of disfellowship the happier he becomes. There does not have to be a known reason for disunity. The existence of it is enough. All who join him stand on the sideline and say forgiveness should not be, it cannot be, the cost is too high and the pain is too great. To these come back the words of the Master, "My grace is sufficient." If one will but obey the call of the Master, forgiveness will not be a beginning, nor will it be an end. Its effectiveness is too great to be stopped by the calls of the world. Its hope is not on the minds of men that only want that which they can get for themselves. Its pleas are for those born of the might and glory of a Savior that cares for all. Its mission is the transformation of lives to be better able to minister to men within the will of Christ.

A person is incomplete without the love of forgiveness. Forgiveness gives relationship to God and Jesus. The lack of it is an indication that one is not in fellowship with himself, God or his brothers. This hampers the design of men to be in fellowship with one another, and without fellowship, there cannot be restoration and reconciliation. The foundation of the Christian is in the power of forgiveness. To take this away is to take away the peace that is available with Jesus. No one can survive without fellowship. A person that says he needs no one and can survive without anyone is not functioning within the greatest capacity that is available to him.

One must take up the cross of Jesus by being repentive of all wrong doings and accept that which is available through forgiveness. With forgiveness one is able to give glory to God. Christ as the head of His church having given Himself to redeem the world should receive glory and praise. To be redeemed is to be forgiven to glorify the Father. Glorification is to be given by man to the Father. Nothing should come between their ability to give in adoration. Christ gave Himself so that one may be able to be preserved in the fellowship to give glory. The Holy Spirit is in agreement with this effort. Christ died and arose, not in hidden splendor, but heightened in glorious splendor to be renewed by the Holy Spirit. The Holy Spirit is the source upon which every believer, as a part of the ministry of God under the anointing of Him, is to be known. As such, one is a part of the glorious assembly without spots or wrinkles. It is a principle upon which every man or woman can be a part of through fellowship and restoration. Christ made provisions for this with a full and complete work through redemption. This redemption gives supreme joy upon the final turn on this earth to be in glorious fellowship with Christ in heaven forever more. It will be worth it all to see the face of Jesus as the light of "glory" and of love.

There is no process or intensity within the power of man that allows him freedom to make radical decisions against his possessions for the welfare and good of another. It just does not happen! Nor is there within the mind of man the availability of knowledge that says to him, give up your pride and self-will for a lasting relationship. Therefore, it must be acknowledged that there is a power and source far greater than man. There must be the need to feel and have this power within to guide one in the path of righteousness.

Throughout this chapter the emphasis has been on the Holy Spirit. The Holy Spirit is not an it or a thing. Man is influenced by things based upon the power and prestige they bring to him. The Holy Spirit as a part of the divine authority must be thought of as a person. Recognition must again be given to the heavenly Father through Jesus Christ on what He is capable of doing. There is no magical or mystical force that can be called at will. This is a person that is better than the one in which He dwells. When someone dwells, there is the distinction of residing, lingering and making himself at home. The Holy Spirit loves being within a man. Being within, He establishes fellowship and guides one to grow in truth and under this leadership He must lead and provide guidance for the process of forgiveness. He knows that all are not on the same plane and that the direction chosen for one may be different from another.

He does not bend on truth or righteousness. He is committed to justice, yet knows the value of mercy. He extends himself for repented hearts. There is no drawback in His power to help one become the greatest force that is possible in the niche in which he is a part. Gender is not an issue; color and nationality have no virtue with Him. His claim is truth and forgiveness given by the one in which He abides. There is no tomorrow by His will. The presence of Him working and leading is in the present. There is no one greater than Him that led a transformed person from the shackles of sin to freedom in salvation. He is without restriction in love and mercy. He is, in man, the power which causes him to forgive against all odds of the world. Numbers do not sway Him. He is swayed by assurance of a repentant heart. The will of man cannot overpower Him. He is too loving to make man do right. He simply guides him who is in fellowship to His will and purpose. He goes beyond the standards of the world and He has come to guide, and lead all to truth. This is the influence which man must be a part of to continue the process of forgiveness. Forgiveness is of the divine. It is influenced by the divine and will only act in a divine way within the lives of men and women.

The Holy Spirit has fruit that gives assistance to a person. The ability to forgive is identified in Galatians 5: 22 - 25. Love, joy, peace, patience, kindness, goodness, faithfulness, gentleness, and self-control[1] are essential with forgiveness and makes reconciliation easier. When a person forgives another he or she becomes submissive to the power of the Holy Spirit and the fruit of the Spirit becomes more dominant in daily living. Forgiveness is the will of God and when displayed, it allows a person to grow in the grace and glory of Jesus Christ. Reconciliation then becomes a reality through the fruit of the Spirit, wherein the flesh is crucified with its passion and desires.

CHAPTER 10

The Joy of Forgiveness

Doing right brings inner joy and peace. There is within the process of forgiveness a wholesome and liberating act which releases joy. This joy brings peace to the inner man which allows him to express contentment. It gives freedom to the person that commits wrong to have joy. This also allows one's character to move above the plane of guilt, shame and hatred to a positive self-identity with love.[18]

When joy is vacant in one's life, he cannot enjoy the fullest praise that the heavenly Father has for him. The plea must go out, "Restore unto me the joy of thy salvation." Psalm 51:12. Joy brings an awareness of the touch of the sun, the bloom of a flower, the sunset, a cool breeze on a summer day and misty rain in dry heat, with freedom to enjoy and appreciate each. It denounces worthlessness and creates wholeness in a relationship through Christ with his fellow man.

Joy allows one to see what one is able to accomplish without the restrictions that non-forgiveness brings. The whole man needs to be able to worship God with freedom and serve him by using every part of his body in adoration. Joy serves to bring the willingness so that mercy and humbleness function at their greatest height. Joy can and should be made complete. Without complete joy, there is not a complete man. Forgiveness provides for the recipient of wrong deeds, and the one guilty of committing the wrong deeds to be at peace with each other in the completeness of joy.

In the song, "Joy Unspeakable" by B. E. Warner from the scripture I Peter: 1:8, "Whom having not seen, ye love; in whom, though now ye see him not, yet believing, ye rejoice with joy unspeakable and full of glory."[2] The forgiveness from one brother to another allows grace to be complete as one continues to learn at the feet of Jesus. Forgiveness gives pleasure and peace within. Forgiveness as a blessing allows one to be saved from the awful gulf of sin. Forgiveness is hope in the realm of grace. It is joy from the inside out springing up within the forgiven soul. It is joy unspeakable and full of Glory.

It is to the advantage of the offended person to extend forgiveness, and the person committing the act to receive forgiveness. Through this process each person will be able to claim the joy available through the grace of Jesus. A repented person has access to joy while a forgiving person assures the success of joy. No one loses, no one wins, and each accepts the grace that is available from the Master's table.

The joy of forgiveness gives one the opportunity to worship with the Lord without restriction. This process gives one the freedom to be open to the Holy Spirit. Joy of forgiveness opens a pathway of love for the outcast and broken-hearted. This allows for harmony instead of disharmony, and love instead of hate and bitterness. The reuniting of two people after much hatred and bitterness is accomplished with love and joy. The joy of forgiveness is not what one has obtained or not obtained on the outside, it is what one has become on the inside.

Joy is not to be determined by a smile or lack of it. It is not limited to the receiving of gifts, nor does it elevate itself over personal accomplishments. Joy is the full substance of what one is when he chooses to do what is correct versus what is wrong. There is a commitment to follow the principles of righteousness rather than those that penetrate the mind to do that which is wrong.

The fulfillment of joy for any person is knowing that he is in the fellowship with Jesus, being aware that within the fellowship there is unity through the process of forgiveness which provides joy. This is not an imagination of what can be; it is the reality of what is. It cannot be rewarded for what one has accomplished or what one hopes to accomplish. The expression of joy allows one to know that there is something deep and wonderful that is not established by money.

There is no time for joy to be conquered. The ability of it involves the internal being of one to reach beyond selfish desires to help another to achieve unexpected goals. Joy is conquered by giving of one's self to be the best that God wants him to be. The best is the plan of salvation. That is to live within the mercy and love that is available through forgiveness. With forgiveness comes thanks and appreciation. The combination of these enhances the relationship with Christ to stimulate joy to make it pertinent with forgiveness. Joy is an expression of the glorious favor that one has in achieved relationships. It satisfies the mind and heart of the body to be relaxed at the outcome of a relationship.

There is no will to have joy and place it on display for having achieved certain awards or goals. It is within the boundaries of joy to be open, honest and grateful. Joy does not have time to be deceived into thinking it is something that it is not. It is an expression through the lives of people that gives freedom. Joy, for the most part, is an end result that comes from good and bad situations. Joy brings inner peace.

When a person is in the habit of committing wrong deeds, there cannot be any joy. Sinful deeds stop or hamper the flow of joy. The design of joy is not to be exhibited within the desires of doing that which is wrong. Joy is for the one that does what is right. Righteousness invokes joy. Joy may not be a happy experience as one is experiencing pain. Yet there is a greater hope beyond pain and suffering when one experiences the love and fellowship of Jesus.

Joy is not restricted or limited to peace. When one is faced with the problems of life with mental pain, joy can continue to be a profound emotion. This would suggest joy can be within a person when he is facing serious problems. The experience of the pain may not sit well, but a person knowing whom he serves may overcome and endure a situation void of joy.

Joy may not release pain or disappointment. It makes facing the problems so much better, and it gives a person something to hope for and hang on to. It has been said by someone, "Behind every cloud and rain the sun is still shining." Behind every painful experience is the opportunity to become better than before. Troubled times will come and go. The big thing is knowing that strength and help is available as one stands in pain.

Joy is demonstrated in many ways - when a baby is born into a family or a child completes high school or college. There is joy when one is recognized for doing a good deed such as rescuing someone from a fire or providing assistance for an injured person. The list goes on with people having experienced joy for whatever reason appropriate to them.

There is a joy that is available without the yell or the excited heartbeat in appreciation for the moment. It is the kind that is exhibited in situations that involves other people. When events are unwarranted and the complaints come in, when no one seems to be listening or caring about one's problem, the internal body must be able to say, "I cannot change this, there is nothing I can do about it, so my best effort is to go forward doing all that I can." When a person does this, that is all they can do. People may not change at given times, but the joy of peace allows one to press forward.

In Psalm 51: 1-12, David was made aware of his sins and admitted them. Then he followed with the need for restoration in the fellowship of God. Sin has blocked the relationship that was so vital through the process of forgiveness. David knew this and pleaded that his sin be blotted out and that his heart be made clean. In verse 10, a key word is made of David. He says, "Renew a right spirit within me."[2] "Renew" would suggest that at one time there was some joy and a binding relationship until sin occurred in the life of David. He lost joy, salvation and the freedom of peace. In verse 12 the words were made with the need of restoration. "Restore unto me the joy of thy salvation; and uphold me with thy free spirit."[2] With restoration comes joy and happiness. For David this was not enough, so he requested more power by the words, "uphold me with thy free spirit." There is a joy that comes from God in the favor of salvation under the anointing of the Holy Spirit. There are no drawbacks because the flow of joy is controlled by God. If one is to receive it, there are established roles and conditions that one must adhere to. Even as king, David was not excluded from obeying God's words. To obey God is to have joy; to disobey him is to be void of joy.

The greatest thing David had available to him was the process of forgiveness. Forgiveness warrants joy. One definition of joy is to experience or show pleasure. In verse 14 of Psalm 51, David states, "Deliver me from bloodguiltiness, O God, thou God of my salvation: and my tongue shall sing aloud of thy righteousness."[2] In joyful appreciation and pleasure David noted that he would "sing aloud of righteousness." The praise would not be a whisper or thought of the mind. Loudness here is that David is happy and elated with the restoration that is worthy of being known.

As one gives honor to God, there is a fruit of the spirit which is joy. When one lives within the spirit, there is the need to work in the spirit. Walking within the spirit of God brings one to the reality that there is glory through the manifestation with the process of forgiveness. When forgiveness is accepted, there is a binding force of two in a joyous relationship. The relationship helps two people - the one giving, and the one receiving.

In a relationship between people, the binding force that continually holds them together is love. Love does not prevent problems form surfacing. Love holds two people together during problems. There is no blaming or pointing fingers at the cause of the problem. With love there is respect for the giving of oneself for the welfare of others. There is no demanding or rights or favors. Joy is the settlement of the relationship. With joy, contentment is at the surface of the relationship. One is happy because the other person thought enough to have him as a partner in fellowship. Love thrives on fellowship. It does not seek to achieve everything in life for itself at the expense of others. To have love is to have joy. To have joy is to have a spirit of happiness within one's soul. In the song, Joy Unspeakable, by Barney E. Warren, he states, "I have found a hope so bright and clear living in the realm of grace; O the Savior; presence is so near, I can see his smiling face. It is joy unspeakable and full of glory. O, the half has never been told." Barney Warren knew that living in the grace given by Jesus and accepting grace for what it was that there was some joy that could not be explained. The joy that was available was because of the presence of the Savior. Love brings the presence of the Lord into relationships. Joy is fulfilled in the agreement of one or more persons to do that which is right. When righteousness is not part of a relationship, the joy of the Lord is not there and the relationship cannot function at the highest level that is void of love.

All too often the relationship of people is void of fellowship because forgiveness has not been given for wrong deeds committed. When forgiveness is not within broken relationships, the opportunity for being mended is going to be hard to reach. When forgiveness is given in the place of revenge for recognized wrongs and willful deeds, love becomes a part of the forgiving process. Then when the feeling of loss seems to be too great, joy adjusts one to feel content to doing what was right. There remains in one's mind the damages incurred, yet the power of joy melts the urge of bitterness.

When a child does wrong, the repeated acts of doing wrong allows the parents to discipline the child. No joy for the child may be experienced in the discipline, nor may the parent feel happy in the discipline of the child. Each time the child deviates from the established law of the home, discipline must be given with love. As the child grows to maturity, there is the need to turn him over to Jesus with prayer and trust that he will be taken care of by Him. Doing this provides joy for the parent knowing that God loves the child more than they, and He too will discipline as deemed necessary. Peace and joy carries the parent to new levels in depending on God. He is able to accomplish that which a parent cannot even with all their parenting skills.

In St. John, chapter 15, verse 11, these words are found: "These things have I spoken unto you, that my joy might remain in you, and that your joy might be full."[2] Jesus was the author of joy for the disciples with faith and fruits, as they abided within his will. The joy of the Lord is available to be in the highest perfection. It is to be in combination with love and filled to its greatest capacity. This joy is not a shadow of what one may hope to receive; it is beyond restrictions. It is from Jesus Christ and satisfies one's soul. This joy, which comes from Christ, is not misdirected by the evil of the world. It is not for the world to give, for that which the world gives does not fulfill. It does not give peace of mind and solitude, there remains a lodging for satisfaction. With Jesus there is a joy permeated from heaven that radiates in the lives of men and women to bring satisfaction for the daily routines of life. There is happiness and rejoicing through the joy given by Jesus. He is pleased with all that takes up joy and makes it a part of life. There is agreement of this joy by the Father, Son and Holy Spirit. It is without fault, failure and most important, it does not leave one void and empty.

Jesus is joy. He wants followers of Him to be filled with joy. This joy is not for sinners; it cannot be available until there is the acknowledgement of sin and a request for forgiveness. Since Jesus is joy, the one that is a part of Him is attached to the joy which He displaces. Joy is to the Father as fruit is to the tree. Fruit taken from the tree is refreshing and joy from the Master is also refreshing. Without the Master there is no joy. Without the tree there is no fruit. Fruit is not dependent upon its own source of power. Without being attached to the tree by way of the branches, the fruit dies. The same goes for joy that is not attached to Jesus. It is available through the love that God has for every man. When the love is broken by the wariness of man, a separation is in effect, that is without power from the Master. The only difference is that forgiveness is in effect for man to redeem himself repeatedly back to Jesus. Jesus has pledged himself for man. The very nature of Jesus is to offer love and forgiveness for sin. When man accepts this grace of mercy with love, he is on a road of reconciliation. From reconciliation to restoration, man is in fellowship which earns glory and praise from the Master.

What is it about joy that makes it so valuable in one's life? To have joy is to abide in Jesus. Abiding brings contact and consciousness for those that are in sin. With this comes an effort to make people aware of the blessings that are available through the love of Jesus. As one is forgiven of sin, there is a need to help others experience the forgiveness of sin and enjoy the joy of the Lord. With joy comes strength for a journey that only Jesus can serve as the leader. There is an awareness that as one journeys there are definite steps to be taken. Not knowing how high or low the steps of life are, there is no other hope except to abide with Jesus. When one abides in Jesus, there is recognition of personal weakness. In this way, the Holy Spirit can lead and guide with the assurance that as it works, God is working. God's work is of a divine nature and there is joy in the Lord when He sees one of his children operating by the promises that are available through Him. As long as a person abides in Jesus, he remains faithful to the cause that he is nothing and Jesus is all. To be all is inclusive of the attributes of Jesus. All of Jesus is pure. His righteousness is pure. Whatever he deems to occur is within His divine revelation. No one can control or change it.

With victory, there is joy that makes the heart merry. A heart that is glorious and merry is one that can be at peace and be of good cheer to others. When there is no longer a void in one's heart because of hate and bitterness, the joy of the Lord is able to bring light that illuminates one's life. Joy becomes a radiant gesture that is visible for others to see. Joy of the Lord is real, and those people that come in contact with the person that has joy will know it to be the real thing.

Why? Because joy is not built on a broken fellowship with God. It is manifold with blessings on an unbroken relationship with the Master. It is designed for happiness and pleasure. It thrives on success that is pure and in line with the Master's call. Joy allows a person to know love and when necessary, to be love. Joy is not so happy that it ceases to deal with the real world. There are elements of one's life that must be responded to for what the circumstances call for. A person with joy does not live in a sense of blindness when issues and decisions need to be made. Joy is of the Master because it comes from Him. As such, it has no need to be misdirected. It deals with simple facts and issues to be resolved in simple truths. God is truth. He who abides in Him is truth. God is holy and His joy is also holy. What a great combination - a holy God with a holy joy! Both are available for the pleasure of anyone that will heed the call of God.

Joy provides a more abundant life. One without joy cannot be better off than the person that has it. Joy makes one better than before. There is newness in life that is richer and sweeter. With joy, bad attitudes become good attitudes. Bad speech becomes words of kindness and gratitude, and joy gives a person the foundation of pleasure that can only come from God. It allows one to reach out to others in forgiveness. When the opportunity presents itself, wherever it is needed, joy offers forgiveness through the love that God has for sinners. When a sinner changes his way of living to accept the way of Jesus, there is joy for the heavenly host. One that was lost can join in with praise and joy to sing, "God is great and worthy to be praised." Praises before the Lord is a time for joy to be radiant. A happy time of praise with God is all joy. To be in a relationship with another will only last for a season. Death eventually takes the life of those that have radiated joy. With the Lord, joy is forever. This joy is only for those that are in fellowship with Him.

When a person faces problems and is not sure of what to do, there must be a relationship with Jesus as they seek to solve these problems. As wonderful as joy is, there is the need to know that joy does not solve problems. It is one of the fruits of the Spirit. There is a specific function that is maintained of which it is responsible. The death of Christ on the cross cannot occur again. The price has been paid in full. Joy cannot sidetrack this great deed. Joy can and should be a part of the process of forgiveness. When the process is in action, joy enters in to give one an open mind and the freedom of pleasure. As one opens his mouth to confess his sins, there is joy from the Heavenly Father knowing that one of His children is returning home. Joy is not the end result. It is one of the ways to be used as a sign of fellowship with Jesus.

It should be worth noting that joy does not come because things are going well. A person may have all the money he desires and all the things that money could purchase, and not have joy. Joy, therefore, is not dependent upon things. There are many people that are without joy even though they are financially secure. How is it that a person can have all the power, money and fame, and be void of happiness that comes from joy? Man has within him the need to be in a relationship with Jesus. He can disregard this or heed it and establish a blessed relationship through the process of forgiveness. There is no formula that can be identified to bring on joy that is in the control of man. Man is subjected to the spirit of Jesus with a binding force. The heart of a man cannot be liberated with things. A man cannot purchase or implant joy to another through good. People walk away from security of money. They leave jobs that do not offer fulfillment after many years of investing time. People have worked in key roles for years only to state that they were never happy. Even in marriages many spouses have stated that there was never any joy experienced in the relationship. Why do people seek to have joy at such a high price? There is a need to have something in life that is missing that brings internal happiness. Things do not last, marriages fail, positions come and go, and all without joy. Joy is available in each of these situations, and a person could receive this joy. Joy that is of the Lord does not come to make things bad. Its influence may be felt in the worse situations, and it is felt when things are going well. The forces of good and evil found on the outside do not influence joy to act on the inside. That which is outside remains the crutch that causes so much pain to the point that he can say, "No devil or anyone can steal my joy." It is too valuable, too dynamic to be twisted in things to be ineffective. When a person has joy, it is of a supernatural calling to bring happiness and peace in spite of all the terrible things going on around a person.

When others around are falling into dismay and gloom, joy helps one to elevate above the problem. All too often a person becomes a part of the problem, thereby hindering the joy that would be available. If one will only hold to the promise that the Lord will take care of his children, joy will be available when needed. A person must keep in mind that the Lord is a partner in all situations that one may face. He is not there to only make one feel good. He is there to resolve issues and do it through the lives of people. Problems do not kill or affect people. It is only when people allow the problems to dictate what to do that real pain sets in to make matters worse. How sad it is when a person takes his life to get away from problems. This is a sad tragedy with no results except making more pain for those that are left behind to mourn the loss.

Joy brings strength. Joy sees a problem as a problem and not an end. To have life is to have problems. The measurement of a man is how well he copes with those things that he has no control over. All too often people are upset over those things which they have no control. Sleepless nights, loss of weight, no contact with people and no fellowship with Jesus are only a few things that alter one's lifestyle. People also worry about what could occur. To offset this type of behavior, it is of utmost importance that a person has a dynamic daily prayer life. Communication with Jesus causes one not to look at the problem, but to look at Him. He is ready, willing and able to give assistance to those that will heed His plea. "Come unto me all ye that are heavy laden, and I will give you rest." This is not a quick fix or a maybe condition. It is the reality that a source of power is available to anyone who will seek the Master's plea. "Come." There is no call that says one must come. The call is, if one comes, there is rest. What kind of people need to come? Those that are overwhelmed with problems and need the freedom of release with joy stimulated with love. To get this release, people should go to the powerhouse filled with forgiveness.

The greatest fault that hampers joy is the desire to take care of the flesh. This is an impossible task. The more the flesh receives, the more it wants. It never gets enough, it cannot be satisfied. The flesh seeks to do more to get more. There becomes a greater void that the body cannot fill. It may drop from over exertion. It will not listen to sound advice and will not condemn the fleshy desires. In this type of setting, joy cannot flourish. The mind and flesh will not heed the call of the Master and set themselves against him.

Deliverance from this can only come from God by redemption. Redemption will only come when there is recognition of the cross through the blood of Jesus for the forgiveness of sin. A person must believe the word of God about flesh being slain. Only when flesh is crucified with Christ will one be able to experience joy. Romans 6:6 states: "Knowing this, that our old man is crucified with him."[2] When that which is old has never been crucified with Christ, there is hope and aspiration of joy.

Galatians 5:24 states: "And they that are Christ's have crucified the flesh with the affections and lusts."[2] If one is to have control over the flesh, he must be in a relationship with Christ and be submissive to him. By being submissive to him, Christ crucifies the flesh. As long as man remains in Christ's flesh, he is under the power of God and is controlled by Him. Without the power of God, flesh is an enemy and out of control. With Jesus Christ there is control, understanding, love, peace and joy. All of these are necessary for one to have strength to be an over comer. Each day, step by step, one walks in the pathway of duty before the Master. As one walks, Jesus provides what is needed to be in constant fellowship with Him. Through His spirit, with love and care, man can make it to be the best that he can be. God wants the best for everyone. He gave His best for the world and in return He wants the best from man. The only way a man can be at his best is to be in Jesus. There is no other way. Jesus is the answer for man's release from bondage through the flesh. Joy waits to give happiness with peace of mind for those that are in fellowship with the Master. Through the love of the Master flesh can become submissive. Christ must be the drive for flesh to go to the right place and respond to the word. To be in control of flesh there must be a belief that Jesus died on the cross and in him there is truth. With truth comes joy which radiates all that is needed for renewed and continual fellowship. Man cannot expect any assistance from the world. If the world had the answer, there would not be any need for Jesus. I John 5:5-7 states, "Who is he that overcometh the world, but he that believeth that Jesus is the Son of God? This is he that came by water and blood, even Jesus Christ; not by water only, but by water and blood. And it is the spirit that beareth witness, because the spirit is truth. For there are three things that bear record in heaven, the Father, the Word and the Holy Ghost: and these three are one."[2] Overcoming the world is by believing in Jesus. This does not come cheap. It is by the water and blood which sealed the facts. The resources that validate everything are the Father, Word and Holy Ghost. They perform as one because they are one. These are not lies with the Spirit; the only thing He has to share is the truth. Truth does not need to be validated. It stands alone. Truth in one's life gives joy an opportunity to be its greatest to bring peace. Truth is of God. His very nature is truth. To have fellowship with him is to have truth highlighted with joy.

One must keep in mind that people with key positions and prestige may receive the approval of others for a while. When this fails, there must be something on the inside that sustains and keeps others from falling. Approval of others will be lost for a season. When positions are no longer available and popularity is lost, there needs to be an internal peace that keeps one in focus with the Lord. If the heart and mind are set on earthly things without the call of God, disappointment will be the end result. The disappointment will become the focus for failure and self-pity. A person at this point has shifted the focus from where it should be to himself. There is no strength in one's body that allows for dealing and resolving personal complexities of life. The heart of a person must be set on Christ for every need. Therefore, when the positions are no longer available and the rating of approval gets low, being in Christ keeps one going. The life of a person with joy radiates in spite of sorrow.

God is so creative that He takes bad situations and makes them good. He takes the solutions of the world and discards them to having wholeness and happiness. He does not take personal solutions of man and consider them in His will. He does not need the solutions of the world or of man to be creative. God is efficient in solutions. He takes the bad and gives the good for those that are in fellowship with Him. He inspires those that seem hopeless with no direction. He provides laugher where there should be tears of hurt. His solution is with love and care for each individual. No one is forgotten or excluded. He knows the location of each person and offers Himself as a way of getting out of the pitfalls of life to the height of happiness and joy. This is available through the process of forgiveness by confession.

How can joy radiate when there is hurt, hostility, and loss of jobs, friends and family? The key is forgiveness. Forgiveness does not allow the situation to overpower a person in a negative way. Forgiveness brings healing and reverses all the things that would interfere in the restoration of joy. Joy makes the pain, hurt and loss of jobs bearable without affecting daily responsibilities of life.

Forgiveness with joy allows a person to function in all the seasonal changes of life. One cannot control the seasons; they are accepted for what they are. Each has its agenda and creativity. Each has a design of its own. A person has mercy through each season with the goodness of God. To be without the fellowship of God is to be subjected to and by anything that comes with seasonal changes. One needs to keep in mind that God controls life and everything associated with it is locked into the palm of His hands. God only needs to speak to stop anything that comes against His child with the words, "Peace be still." There is consolation knowing that all is well when one is in fellowship with God to face all seasonal changes. Life changes will always go on. They cannot be stopped by the wishes of man. Man can only stand to the side and take whatever comes his way. His only salvation is his strength to face problems with happiness in the Lord Jesus Christ.

The joy of forgiveness provides rejoicing in the Lord. For the Christians as representatives of Jesus, they are to be merciful and show love to a sin-sick world. Being a part of the world is to be a part of a city, country or wherever one may live. This allows for the opportunity to express the joy of the Lord to those that are contacted on a daily basis. As light shines there is no doubt that it is light in darkness, and a person lost in the dark will be guided by the light if he will only follow it. Christians are the light of and to the world, and the world must know without a doubt that Jesus is active in their lives. There is no appeal to sinners by Christians that are without joy. There is no need to appear gloomy, sad or withdrawn from the happy side of life. Jesus seeks to have cheerful people enjoying the happiness of forgiveness as a part of His fellowship.

When a person accepts the Lord, there is always someone that will try to discourage them by reminding them of the things done in the past. Yet, Paul reminds us to press on to the mark of the high calling. One cannot allow anyone to alter the course established by the Master. They must be as persistent as one that picks blackberries. To get to the berries one must avoid the briars and gently remove the berries. In the same like way, when someone comes along to discourage, avoid them and gently pick the things that the

Lord has available in peace and love. A person cannot live in the past. He must live in the present and for the future. There is no worse course of action than mourning over what has taken place in the past. To dwell on the past is to remove and not appreciate the joy of the Master. There is joy and light in Jesus.

One must know where and with whom he stands. There cannot be any doubt in this mater. To have doubt gives Satan a chance to deprive one of what God has already taken care of. One should not even speak with doubt. God is strong and full of mercy. He will not be swayed by the evil spoken of Him, and as Christians there should not be any cause for alarm. God is available and will be for those that put their trust in Him.

It is worth noting again that problems are a part of the life for Christian and sinners. The difference is that Satan will lead one into trouble with no solution for getting out. Jesus leads away from trouble and gives an avenue for escape. There is joy knowing that God is always available to receive praise and glory. Christians should give praises to God because they are a part of the joy of life. People die, hurt, have temptations and may grieve, but the joy of Jesus through praise will bring relief.

Jesus was a man of joy and happiness. It was joy for Him to do the will of the Father. This did not excuse pains and troubles that He had to face. Yet within His experience He had peace, joy and happiness. Man did not crush Him. Nor was He restrained from being the example of a life filled with extending forgiveness. Jesus did not stop joy from thriving in His life. He did not place man in an unwholesome environment that caused him to be without peace and joy. Christ did not come to destroy; He came to bring healing and to minister rather than to be ministered unto by man.

When Jesus was working in the carpentry shop with Joseph, it was certain that things did not go as he pleased, but he was committed to doing the right thing by and for others regardless of their values and feelings for him. When people are committed to doing the things that are right, there will be less worry and confusion for their lives. When one does not know in what direction he is going, he is without vision. With no vision there is no goal or aspirations to seek or obtain. When Solomon needed direction to lead the people, he asked God for wisdom. Wisdom from God allowed him to make wise choices for himself and his people. The wisdom given by God was manifested in the life of Solomon for others to see. With wisdom came knowledge to make daily decisions for the good of the people. When Solomon deviated from the wisdom of God and made bad decisions, he was without the joy of the Lord. God loves and cares too much for his Father and the Spirit to be a part of foolishness. His time is precious and too valuable to give to those that will not accept His call. The best effort for everyone is required at all times. A song has these words, "When you have done your best, let Jesus do the rest, and He will never disappoint your soul." There is no failure in God. With His wisdom one can take care of everything that is needed. Discretion will be dynamic. Excellent results can occur because He knows all and everything that exists is not without His knowledge. The cases of the world and those of an individual are too extensive to be handled by anyone but God.

With God in control, His will shall be the focus to bring all to be over comers. The zones of danger that are prepared to defeat will be avoided through the trust and care of God. With God's care, provision is offered to all that will accept it. None of His children will have to beg for bread. They only need to work in the joy of the strength that has been given by

God to obtain bread. A lazy person will not make it and has no place with God. There is joy in working to provide for the basic needs of life. With honor and glory a man is wise to use the hands that God gave to be worthy of his hiring.

God takes care of His own. What a joy to know that there is someone who stands at the gate of needs to fill them according to his riches in glory. Matthew 6:28: "And why take ye thought for raiment? Consider the lilies of the field, how they grow; they toil not, neither do they spin."[2] Verse 29: "And yet I say unto you, That even Solomon in all his glory was not arrayed like one of these."[2] God is able to take care of each person as He cared for the lilies. They grow receiving nourishment without the sweat of labor and they are better than Solomon's temple. Why? Because Solomon had his temple built to his specifications. But the lilies grow to the specification that the Master has provided. They grow in contentment of the Master's will and care. People are not less than the lilies. God rates them above flowers. As He provided for them, so must He provide for His children with love. He does it with joy and happiness. As He extends joy in working with man to be the best, man in turn receives joy and reciprocates it to his peers. There is peace and joy in the Lord today and His praises should ring across the world. Happy is he that is in the will of the Father because He cares for thee. Happy is he who receives the wisdom of Jesus to go forward with satisfaction in a relationship of peace and love.

Every person needs the joy of forgiveness which brings one into a sphere of communion with Christ. With communion there is love that is present through the fellowship of being in Christ. Then the spirit brings guidance that brings one into a deeper relationship with the Lord. One that is on the right path brings honor and devotion for the mercy given by God to a repentant heart. As one gets closer to Christ there is prayer of adoration and comfort. There is in Him a cup waiting to be flowing over with all the things needed for the journey with the Master. Psalm 23:5 states: "Thou preparest a table before me in the presence of mine enemies: thou anointest my head with oil; my cup runneth over."[2] A table that is prepared by the Master is a royal divine treat. It will not be done behind closed doors, it will be visible to the eyes of enemies and they will not be able to deter it in any manner. Oil, sweet smelling oil over the head, not just poured on it, but the oil shall be anointed by Jesus. The inner man shall be filled to the top. It will not stop, but continually run over. More than enough is the will of the Father. Not just enough love, or peace, joy and mercy, but enough for the receiver to share with someone. The receiver becomes the receiver and giver of good things for those around him. A change of attitude, a changed life visible for others to see is joy in the recognition that all is well with Jesus.

In a small cell meeting a member told of a personal experience she had gone through and how she was going to keep quiet. But she decided to share with the group. She had a person come to her in need of some money which she did not have. For the welfare of the other person, she borrowed the money and gave it to the other person. She was told the money would be repaid and she in turn would pay off the loan. Later she discovered that the other person had left town, address unknown. She was let down, frustrated, and hurt because she performed a deed in good faith to meet a need. Instead of getting bitter, she prayed for the other person, accepted the loss, and started repaying the loan. She never wished ill for the other person, but in her daily prayer she prayed for the best to occur and in the spirit of prayer she offered forgiveness of what the other person had done to her. "Never once did I feel sorry for myself for having to start repaying the loan. And all the time I repaid the loan, I asked the Lord to forgive and I have love for the other person. And right now, I have joy with Jesus down in my heart." Later the sister received a long distance call from the other person acknowledging wrong and promising that they would send all the money back to her. By this time the group was overcome with joy over the way the Lord moved with the sister through sharing her experience. There was a great discovery for many within the group that heard how the Lord moved. There is happiness in people when they can observe through life what forgiveness is about.

The sister wanted to keep quiet, but through her sharing, the gleam in her eyes and the glow of her face gave proof that the forgiveness offered was real. The process of hurt and loss was not denied. But the most important thing above all else was the love she had for Jesus, herself and the other person that continued with prayer. To release one from the debt say, "You are free because my salvation is worth too much to hold someone when Jesus has released me from sin." Joy did not ease itself into the testimony of the sister. It was a part of the choices that were made to tell and allow others to know that it can be done. Forgiveness works, love works, and thy can be apparent in the lives of people. To go through an experience and come out on top with losses, hurt and anger, yet retain the love of Jesus, is worth all the joy that one can experience. Joy is available through troubled times because joy is of God. As one experiences the joy of doing the right thing, there is happiness that at times cannot be vocalized. Tears of joy at overcoming the world situation is for the best. Joy may be looked upon as being crazy, but for the person in the situation, it is the test of the soul, mind and body. It is not to be kept, but it is to be told for others to share with gladness. Good news is worth others knowing about. It is of no importance unless it is shared with others.

When one goes through the process of forgiveness and offers the elements of love, peace, good tidings and mercy, God is at work not to the credit of the person, but to the one who is able to keep His will. The process of forgiveness begins before the act. With the act it is brought to conclusion. With the process, there are questions to be answered, bitterness to be banned, anger to be made without hate, loses to be released without payment, and hurt with pain to be acknowledged. Yet the process is worth it all in that the process validates the act. How can one reach a conclusion without processing the what, where, when and how? It does not make the person smaller, nor does it take anything away. Forgiveness with joy stays within the process already approved, experienced and concluded with Christ on the cross.

There is no other way by which one person can release another except by forgiveness. The experience of joy makes it worthwhile for one having gone through the temptation of Satan. It is wrong to hate, get even, laugh at reciprocal trouble and predict future trouble for wrong acts committed against the offended person. Such actions are not the way of the Lord. James 1:2 states: "My brethren, count it all joy when ye fall into divers temptations."[2] Troubled times will come for all that do the will of the Lord. Darkness may come as one seeks the light of help as if it is not always available from the Father. The inner self must stand still and know that the God of all is at work from the past, in the present and for the future. Sunshine one day and clouds the next does not deactivate God. He is always available in the Trinity. They work as one unified to help each person that is in fellowship to do their will.

Trouble does not come to tear down, but to build up. Faith is not tried so that it can be conquered; rather it extends itself to Him that keeps all. Waves of life are not washed deeper into the depth of the ocean of being forgotten. It is to show that where the debt is located, there is Jesus. Evil is not to conquer, but to be placed at the feet of Jesus who is the conqueror. Tests of life are set to prove what one's call is about. It leaves no time for finding fault. It accepts with contentment that all is well with anyone that abides in fellowship with the Master.

Joy is not for those that give up and say it is no use. It does not adorn itself at one that has self-pity. It does not seek to make matters worse. Joy gives life a glow and radiates from within to the outside. It has no solution, but keeps to Him who has all the solutions. With joy, love is an expected behavior. Joy gives foundation to the process of forgiveness. There is a better feeling as one forgives self to receive forgiveness of the Father with joy. As one forgives others, the freedom of joy is allowed to be invited into one's heart for doing the right thing. It is not phony when joy is felt, because joy is of a divine call, and joy enters a body that is alive to the will of salvation. With joy there is no perfection, it is the will of the Father. As great as pain can be, joy supersedes and outshines pain in the process of time. "For God so loved that He gave." Any child of God must so love that giving is a normal way of activating love. As Jesus forgave, so must all that seeks to do His will and receive His favor. The Holy Spirit gives the assistance when and where needed. Distance and speed are not a problem. He loves to guide that which is righteous. Joy seals the approval of righteousness and love allows all who will to draw of the foundation of salvation with happiness. To have happiness is to have joy.

NOTES

1. The Holy Bible: New American Standard. (United States of America: Moody Press. 1975).
2. The Holy Bible: Authorized King James Version. (United States of America: World Book Publishing, Inc., 1989).
3. Ruthie Byer, and Lawrence D. Pruitt, Evening Light Song. (Oklahoma: Faith Publishing House, 1965), 209.
4. Charles Spurgeon, Morning and Evening. (Pennsylvania: Faith Publish House, 1992), 667.
5. Ruth Peal, Positive Thinker Club. (Pawling, New York: Peal Center for Christian Living, 1999), 1-4.
6. David Augsburger, The Freedom of Forgiveness 70 x 70. (Chicago: Moody Press, 1978), 27.
7. Lewis B. Smedes, Forgive and Forget. (San Francisco: Harper & Roe Publisher, 1984), 9.
8. Lewis B. Smedes, Forgive and Forget. (San Francisco: Harper & Roe Publisher, 1984), 124.
9. David Augsburger, Caring Enough to Forgive. (Kichener, Ontario: Herold Press, 1991), 29-37.
10. David Augsburger, Caring Enough to Forgive. (Kichener, Ontario: Herold Press, 1991), 21.
11. Henry Matthew, Commentary on the Whole Bible. (Grand Rapids, Michigan: Zandervan Publishing House, 1969), 1498.
12. John F. McArthur, The Freedom and Power of Forgiveness. (Wheaton, Illinois: Crossway Books, 1998), 240.
13. David Augsburger, Caring Enough to Forgive. (Kitchener, Ontario: Herold Press, 1991) 21.

14. Hogue T. Wilson, The Holy Spirit. (Shoals, Indiana: Schmal Publishing Company, 1998), 115-130.
15. Ray Simmons, Commentary on Luke. (Waco, Texas: World Book Publishers, 1972), 184-185.
16. Hogue T. Wilson, The Holy Spirit. (Shoals, Indiana: Schmal Publishing Company, 1998) 121.
17. Alan Richardson, An Introduction to the Theology of the New Testament. (New York: Harper & Row Publishers, 1958), 123.
18. John F. MacArthur, The Freedom and Power of Forgiveness. (Wheaton, Illinois: Crossway Books, 1998), 1975.

BIBLIOGRAPHY

Augsburger, David, Caring Enough to Forgive. Kichener, Ontario: Herold Press, 1991.

Byer, Ruthie and Pruitt, Lawrence D, Evening Light Song. Guthrie, Oklahoma: Faith Publishing House, 1965.

Chadwick, Samuel, The Way to Pentecost. Washington, Pennsylvania: Christian Crusade, 1956.

Henry, Matthew, Commentary on the Whole Bible. Grand Rapids, Michigan: Zandervan Publishing House, 1969.

King James Version, The Holy Bible. United States of America: World Book Publishing, Inc., 1989.

New American Standard, The Holy Bible. United States of America: Moody Press, 1975.

McArthur, John F., The Freedom and Power of Forgiveness. Wheaton, Illinois: Crossway Books, 1998.

Peale, Ruth, Positive Thinker Club. Pawling, New York: Peal Center for Christian Living, 1999.

Pentecost, Dwight J., The Word and Work of Jesus Christ. Grand Rapids, Michigan: Zanderan Publishing House, 1981.

Richardson, Allan, An Introduction of the Theology of the New Testament. New York: Harper & Roe.

Simmons, Ray, Commentary on Luke. Waco, Texas: World Book Publishers, 1972.

Smedes, Lewis B., Forgive and Forget. San Francisco: Harper & Roe Publisher, 1984.

Spurgeon, Charles, Morning and Evening. New Kensington, Pennsylvania: Whitaker House, 1991.

Wilson, Hogue T., The Holy Spirit. Shoals, Indiana: Schmal Publishing Company, 1998.

About the Author

Bernard Kent Jr. was born in Savannah, Georgia and graduated from Savannah State College in 1965 with a Bachelor's degree in Science. He later attended Warner Pacific in Portland, Oregon and graduated Cum Laude in 1978 with a Master's of Religion. On August 11, 2000, he received a Doctorate of Religion degree from Covington Theological Seminary in Rossville, Georgia from which he again graduated Cum Laude.

Dr. Kent has received numerous awards and accolades including Who's Who Among America's Teachers and Teacher of the Year for Effingham County Public Schools. He is active in the Savannah Church of God where he has been a member for many years.

Dr. Kent is the oldest of three children born to Reverend Bernard Kent Sr. and Mrs. Ludene Kent. He has two sisters, Mrs. Elise Green and Mrs. Bettie Cannon. Bernard is the Father of four children Schenterial, Sharnda, Absolon (Al), and Berneta. He also has eight grandchildren, Jasmine, Brittany, BreAnna, Alberto, Trenton, Mileak, Malcolm, and Matthias (Matty). Forgiveness: A Process, Not an Act is his first published book.

www.ingramcontent.com/pod-product-compliance
Lightning Source LLC
LaVergne TN
LVHW091009080826
845145LV00003B/1199

* 9 7 8 0 9 8 1 4 6 5 0 1 2 *